Touring Niagara Wine Country

Second Edition

Linda Bramble

JAMES LORIMER & COMPANY LTD., PUBLISHERS
TORONTO

© 2003 Linda Bramble

James Lorimer & Company Ltd. acknowledges the support of the Ontario Arts Council. We acknowledge the support of the Government of Canada through the Book Publishing Industry Development Program (BPIDP) for our publishing activities. We acknowledge the support of the Canada Council for the Arts for our publishing program. We acknowledge the support of the Government of Ontario through the Ontario Media Development Corporation's Ontario Book Initiative.

All photography by Dwayne Coon except pages:
81, 83, 87, 92, 93, Wine Council Of Ontario & Steve Elphick
Design and layout: Gwen North
Maps: Peggy McCalla

National Library of Canada Cataloguing in Publication
Bramble, Linda
    Touring Niagara wine country / Linda Bramble. — 2nd ed.
Includes index.
ISBN 1-55028-795-8
                1. Niagara Peninsula (Ont.)—Guidebooks. 2. Niagara
Peninsula (Ont.)—Tours. 3. Wineries—Ontario—Niagara
Peninsula—Guidebooks.
I. Title.
FC3095.N5B72 2003   917.13'38044   C2003-903624-3

James Lorimer & Company Ltd.,
Publishers
35 Britain Street
Toronto, Ontario
M5A 1R7
www.lorimer.ca

Distributed in the U.S. by
Casemate
2114 Darby Road, 2nd floor
Havertown, PA
19083

Printed and bound in Canada

CONTENTS

MAP

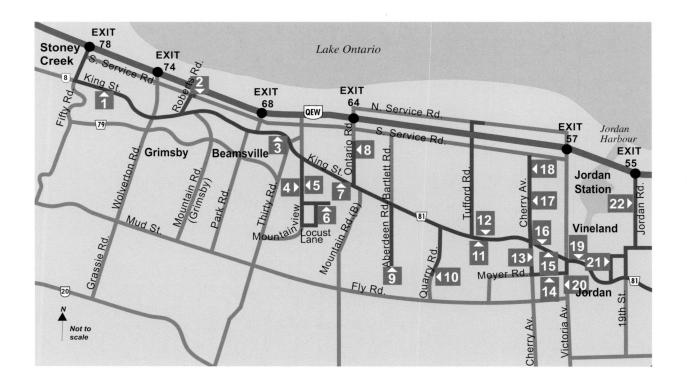

Key to locations on map

1. Puddicombe Estate
2. Kittling Ridge
3. Peninsula Ridge Estates
4. Angels Gate Winery
5. Thirty Bench Vineyard and Winery
6. EastDell Estates
7. Daniel Lenko Estate Winery
8. Magnotta Beamsville
9. Crown Bench Estates
10. De Sousa Wine Cellars
11. Malivoire Wine Company
12. Thomas and Vaughan Vintners
13. Lakeview Cellars
14. Vineland Estates
15. Kacaba Vineyards
16. Willow Heights Estate Winery
17. Royal de Maria
18. Birchwood Estate Wines
19. Stoney Ridge Cellars
20. Featherstone Estate Winery and Vineyard
21. Cave Spring Cellars
22. Harbour Estates Winery

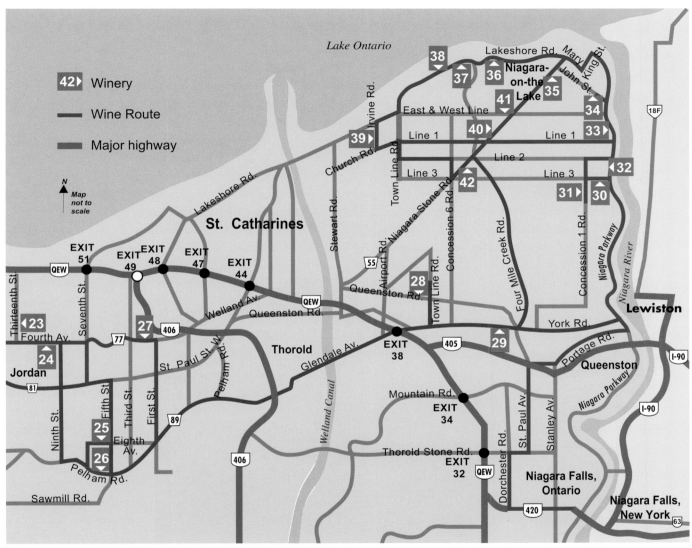

23. Thirteenth Street Winery
24. Creekside Estate Winery
25. Hernder Estate Wines
26. Henry of Pelham Family Estate Winery
27. Harvest Estates Wines
28. Maleta Vineyards and Estate Winery
29. Château des Charmes

30. Inniskillin Wines
31. Marynissen Estates
32. Reif Estate Winery
33. Lailey Vineyards
34. Peller Estates Winery
35. Jackson-Triggs Vintners
36. Sunnybrook Farm Estate Winery
37. Strewn Winery

38. Konzelmann Estate Winery
39. Stonechurch Vineyards
40. Pillitteri Estates Winery
41. Joseph's Estate Wines
42. Hillebrand Estates Winery

5

INTRODUCTION: THE NIAGARA PENINSULA

*"If there is one spot intended for paradise ... in point of climate,
soil, variety, beauty, grandeur, and every convenience,
I do believe it is unrivalled."*

Robert Gourlay, 1822

Niagara is a place of transformations — of water into power, of borders into crossroads, of locally grown foods into treasures of the table, of grapes into wine. As a destination, Niagara has meant the Falls, where millions of people are still drawn to their sublime majesty. And, justifiably so. However, because tourists travel through the contemporary express routes of air, road and rail, up until quite recently, they have paid little attention to the striking countryside that makes up the other 99 percent of the peninsula. This book is an invitation to that other Niagara, that stretches 40 kilometres from Grimsby to Niagara-on-the-Lake — through the informality and graciousness of its small, unbesieged towns and villages, to its gentle farms and rolling landscapes, to its waterways and pathways. We will follow the Niagara Wine Route as we prospect for the secret springs of its spirit through this languorous part of Ontario.

The Niagara Peninsula is different from any other place in Canada. Diversity has been its greatest strength. Because of its proximity to power,

A century barn

it became an innovative manufacturing centre, but for the past 200 years, agriculture has accounted for the largest single use of land in the region. In fact, 52 percent of the land is still directed to agriculture. Unlike many localities, farmers here tend to own the property on which they farm. Many are proudly preserved century farms, inherited by sixth-generation families whose ancestors were awarded blocks of land as a result of their loyalty to the British Crown during the American War of Independence. Because of the climate, there are also greenhouses, intensive pork, lamb, poultry, venison and quail operations, as well as a wide variety of field crops such as vegetables, berries and herbs.

This is all possible because of Niagara's location in the northernmost part of the Carolinian Zone, which extends from the U.S. coastal zone of the Carolinas northward. Although Niagara's Carolinian Zone makes up less than one-quarter of 1 percent of Canada's area, it is host to more rare species of plants and animals

Niagara vineyard

than any other region in the nation. Known as the "banana belt of the north," its climate is moderated by the embrace of Lake Erie to the south and Lake Ontario to the north. The Niagara portion of the 765-kilometre Niagara Escarpment forms an East-West spine that is the region's most prominent topographical feature.

So rare and diverse is the ecosystem of the Niagara Escarpment that in 1990 the United Nations named it a World Biosphere Reserve devoted to conservation of nature and scientific research in the service of humanity. It is in this climate (more similar to Burgundy in France than it is to Buffalo in New York, its immediate neighbour to the south) that grapes are able to grow, and it is here that our journey begins.

LANDSCAPE AND CLIMATE

The Niagara Peninsula is situated on the forty-third parallel in Ontario between Lake Ontario to the north and Lake Erie to the south. The moderating influence of these two Great Lakes contributes to a temperate climate similar to growing regions such as Burgundy and the Loire Valley in France, Northern California, Oregon and New Zealand. These cooler regions are subject to the caprices of nature. As if to compensate, wines grown in such temperate climates can produce superior fruit, with better aromas and more intense flavours than in warmer climates.

Lake Ontario has a strong moderating influence on Niagara's northerly location within a distance of 1.5-3 kilometres (.9-1.8 miles) from shore. Spring comes late here, which is good news for vines. A too-warm March can tempt the sap to start flowing through the vines. A frost in April can freeze the sap, causing deadly internal damage from burst vines. This threat is reduced in spring, because warmed air over the land rises, drawing in the cooler lake air, which, in turn cools land tempera-

Tending vines

tures. In winter the pattern is reversed. Summer-warmed water heats the air over the lake, which rises, drawing the cooler early winter air from the land and circulating warmer air over ripening vines. This results in a longer growing season and less severe winters.

The Niagara Escarpment also has an impact on vine growth. It acts like a giant rampart, deflecting the offshore winds. This natural circulation system prevents damaging cold pockets of air from settling in low-lying areas.

MAIN GRAPE VARIETIES
VINIFERS
WHITES

• Chardonnay: Originating in the Burgundy region of France, Chardonnay is Ontario's most planted V. Vinifera white grape. There are oaked as well as unoaked *sur lie* styles exhibiting flavours from crisp apple and melon to pear, grapefruit and peach. Some barrel-aged styles offer rich toffee and vanilla notes. The clone Chardonnay Musqué, seldom oaked, is a more aromatic varietal, crisp with distinctive Traiminer aromas.
• Riesling: This German variety does extremely well in Ontario, producing wines of diverse styles from bone dry with notes of citrus and peach, to very sweet late harvests

and Icewines of honey and tropical fruits such as mangoes, pineapples and melons. Quite distinctive and classic.
• Gewurztraminer: Next in terms of volume produced, Niagara examples show fine character and full body, higher alcohol, intense, assertive typical flavours of rose and lychee nut, ginger and cinnamon.
• Sauvignon Blanc: Quickly gaining ground in Niagara, styles range from aromatic, zesty green fruits such as lime and grapefruit to more tropical, off-dry styles. Some barrel-aged.
• Pinot Gris: Produces soft, slightly pinkish grey wines, usually dry to off-dry. Not as frequently found among producers, but it is doing well, thus encouraging others to plant more.
• Auxerrois: A variety important in Alsace, it produces light wines very similar to Pinot Blanc or an unoaked Chardonnay.

REDS

• Cabernet Franc: the red wine of the Loire Valley and the constituent variety in the blended wines of Bordeaux, does particularly well in Niagara, producing wines ranging from lighter-styled, red berry wines to oaked wines of depth and body.
• Merlot: a slightly later ripener than Cabernet Franc, Merlot does well on suitable sites. Many producers make a varietal wine from Merlot, but more often than not its softer character is blended with Cabernet Sauvignon to emulate the Meritage/Bordeaux styles.
• Cabernet Sauvignon: Although slow to take its place in Niagara, it has been doing increasingly well, thereby filling out the royal Bordelais triumvirate.
• Pinot Noir: French interests from Burgundy (Le Clos Jordan) believe that Niagara is capable of producing world-class Pinot Noir. To that end they have invested heavily in plantings here. The wines produced show the depth and classic character of red berry fruit and the earthiness and rustic elegance of Burgundian styles. This is the red variety to watch.

Merlot grapes

• Gamay Noir: Like Pinot Noir, this other grape from the southern part of Burgundy, Beaujolais, makes wonderfully food-friendly styles from light and fresh cherry to deep and black cherry chocolate. With the development of new clones (Gamay Droit), this could become a signature red for Niagara.

FRENCH HYBRIDS
Although only a limited number are permitted to grow by VQA regulation in Ontario, there are three varietals that show distinction: Vidal, the constituent white variety in many late harvest wines and Icewines; and Baco Noir and Maréchal Foch, both red varieties capable of producing robust wines.

WINE INDUSTRY
Canada is a large country — the second largest landmass in the world, but it is tiny as a wine producer. However,

despite its size, it is capable of producing wines of uncommon excellence. This has not always been the case. The wine industry in Ontario is 175 years old, but just coming of age. Canadian wine, once an oxymoron, is now a model of an industry that has transformed itself from the ground up.

Wine made in Ontario used to come from native grape varieties (V. Labrusca, etc.), which, when fortified made somewhat palatable products; the table wines, however, were most unpleasant. However, a revolution in the Ontario wine industry took place in the mid-seventies, when advances in vineyard management and clonal and rootstock research allowed viticulturists to successfully grow the more distinguished European species of vines (V. Vinifera). Provincial legislation soon forbade the native varieties from being blended into table wines of any sort. To discourage vine growing in areas that produced marginal fruit, and to encourage the development of better-quality wines, a series of measures was taken to elevate the quality of Ontario wines.

In 1988 the vintners of Ontario established the Vintners Quality Alliance (VQA) to define the standards by which Ontario wines of better quality would be recognized. This appellation system formally mapped the better-growing areas and established standards of production. The VQA marque on the bottle allows the consumer to trace and track the origins of the place from which the wine was grown and the standards of production to which it has complied.

VQA

If the label says Product of Ontario:
• All the grapes used in the wine must be grown in Canada with no less than 85 percent from permitted grapes grown in Ontario.
• The wine must meet all VQA standards regarding production(ripeness levels, grape varieties, etc.).
• The wine must be approved by a provincial tasting panel.

If the label indicates one of three specific growing regions (Viticultural Areas: Niagara Peninsula, Pelee Island, Lake Erie North Shore) then:
• All grapes used in the production process must be grown in Ontario from only permitted varieties.
• No less than 85 percent of the wine must originate from grapes in the named VA.
• The wine must meet all standards requirements.
• The wine must be approved by a provincial tasting panel.
• If the label designates a specific vineyard, 100 percent of the grapes in the wine must come from that vineyard.

CUISINE: TASTES OF NIAGARA

Along with vineyards, orchards of cherries, apples, plums, peaches, pears and kiwi complete the rural Niagara landscape. Field crops of tomatoes, beans, carrots and other root vegetables plus berries of every

conceivable variety, also proliferate in summer, making Niagara a cornucopia of fresh produce. The same climate that allows such tender fruits and vegetables to develop concentrated flavours is also conducive to the healthy development of livestock, particularly range chickens and quail, pork, venison, emu and lamb. In addition, located in Niagara is one of the largest system of greenhouses in Canada, many with hydroponic operations, where fresh greens, herbs and vegetables are available nearly year round.

Unique to Niagara is an alliance called "Tastes of Niagara," where local growers work closely with chefs, to grow the produce the chefs want to eventually incorporate into their menus, and provide them with vine and fresh tree-ripened fruit. We are all too familiar with hard-picked, green produce imported from places south that is intended to ripen en route to market. It cannot develop the same ripe flavours of "ripe-picked" products. This guarantee of ripeness provides the tastiest and most nutritious products possible. The high quality of the produce is the most defining characteristic of Niagara's cuisine. Most of the cooking styles of Niagara's better chefs reflect the classic cuisines of Europe; however, the food they serve is the product of their own creativity, highlighted by the pure, ripe flavours of Niagara-grown ingredients.

PLANNING A WINE TOUR

A few simple guidelines to help you get the most out of your visit to wine country.

1. Decide who's going to drive. One person should be designated who will not consume alcohol. Or better yet, hire a driver for the day.

2. Plan to visit no more than four or five wineries a day. Two in the morning, two in the afternoon and one for lunch. More than that and you're rushing. Take the time to enjoy other places of interest that catch your eye along the way.

3. Don't feel you have to drink every ounce you're poured. It's perfectly all right to spit and/or dump out a wine, even if you like it. Tasting bars come equipped with dump buckets. The law in Ontario restricts you to four ounces per winery. That's four, one-ounce samples. Don't expect more. If you swallow everything you're served, by the end of the day you'll be either looped, heading for the sofa for a nap, or nursing a thundering headache.

4. To avoid the latter, snack between visits. Food helps to metabolize alcohol. Don't taste on an empty stomach.

5. To make your tasting experience more complete, avoid wearing perfumed products — colognes, aftershave, perfumed lotions or sun screen — anything with a strong scent. Others around you will thank you for it. Also do not chew gum or candy mints. It will break the winemaker's heart ...

6. Pack a cooler for the wines you buy. Or at the very least cover the wines with newspaper to protect them from cooking in the back seat. Better yet, have them shipped.

7. The beauty of wine touring is that you get to taste wines that are only available at the winery. These are usually in limited supply; so when you find one you like, buy several bottles.

8. To help you remember what you liked and didn't, bring a pocket notebook to record your reactions. As much as you think you'll remember, trust me, jotting down your reactions will do wonders to improve your memory.

9. Have fun!

View from the escarpment

11

GRIMSBY/BEAMSVILLE

pentimento/pentiˈmento:/n. (Pl. **pentimenti**/-ti:/) the phenomenon of earlier painting showing through a layer or layers of paint on a canvas. [Italian=repentance]

GRIMSBY

From Toronto, the Niagara Escarpment starts to dominate the Niagara-bound landscape as the QEW rounds the elbow of the westernmost corner of Lake Ontario near Hamilton. In the distance, its craggy cliffs ribbon their way in obstinate relief to an otherwise uninterrupted plain. For millennia its ridges formed the shoreline of an ancient lake, Lake Iroquois. When the glacier receded, five Great Lakes lingered, with the Escarpment and its fossil-rich layers of sedimentary rock as silent testimony to the shoreline role it once played. Where the ridge skirts the lake at its closest point is our destination — Grimsby.

Grimsby began as a thriving fruit-growing, processing and shipping centre. The first settlers were Americans, loyal to the Crown of England and very disillusioned by the outcome of the American Revolutionary War. As a reward for their loyalty, Britain granted them great tracts of land. The United Empire Loyalists came, cleared, planted and settled the wilderness that was then known as Upper Canada. By the mid-1800s they returned the mother country's generosity by naming their settlement after Grimsby, England, a town once conquered by a Dane named Grim.

Left: *Heritage Home, Grimsby*   Top: *The Farewell House*

13

GRIMSBY

The Good Earth Cooking School
4556 Lincoln Avenue
Beamsville, Ontario, L0R 1B3
Tel: 905-563-7856/1-800-308-5124
Fax: 905-563-9143
www.goodearthcooking.com
The Good Earth is more than just a cooking
school. It's about friendship, learning, making
fond memories with people you care about.
Smack dab in the middle of a 55 acre fruit
farm where proprietor Nicolette Novak spent
her childhood, the cooking school and its
surroundings are a breath of Provence — or
any other place in the world dedicated to
good food and the art of living well.

Classes are limited to twelve participants,
which ensures intimacy and camaraderie. All
classes are designed around what you might
have at home and what is reasonable to
prepare. There is a resident team of chefs
and educators, and Nicolette also invites the
best chefs in Niagara to come and do guest
classes. It's too much fun to miss.

The names of towns and villages, creeks and roads are the pentimenti of the people and events that shaped the evolution of the area. The cardinal names of the major creeks that rise above the Escarpment — The Forty (Grimsby's first name until 1846), The Thirty, The Twenty, The Sixteen, The Twelve and The Four-Mile Creeks — are the pentimenti of British rule, named by the Generals' Surveyors from Fort Mississauga (1760) in Niagara-on-the-Lake, for the distance the creeks were from the mouth of the Niagara River.

Regional Highway 81, the leisurely route through Niagara's wine country on the Escarpment side, was first defined in the 1300s by the Aboriginal people as one of three major trails that crisscrossed Niagara. It is unclear what the Aboriginals called it, but early French and English settlers named it the Iroquois Trail after the Iroquois-speaking tribes who estab-

Forks Road Pottery

lished it as a major trade route to the Great Lakes.

By the time the first Loyalists arrived in the late 1700s with thoughts of emigrating from the unfriendly revolutionary colonies to the south, they found nothing but wilderness. The Native peoples had long been dispersed, conquered and absorbed by other tribes. The dirt path of the Iroquois Trail was soon replaced with planks through more difficult terrain, creating a corduroy road, allowing stage coaches to manoeuvre better through mud and snow.

Other settlements besides Grimsby developed along the same route — inns for travellers and coachmen, pubs for careworn farmers, markets to exchange homemade goods for produce and machinery and churches to console the wilderness-weary families. By the 1900s the trail became known as the No. 8 Highway, part of the King's Highway system in Ontario.

Fork Roads Pottery
53 Ontario Street
Grimsby, Ontario, L3M 3H4
Tel: 905-945-8041
www.forksroad.com
Situated in the century-old train depot is Fork Roads Pottery, where potters combine traditional, functional forms — bean pots, crocks, pitchers, pansy flower rings, bowls, platters, dinnerware with the strength of porcelain. All are oven, microwave and dishwasher safe, with lead-free glazes.

Grimsby Museum
6 Murray Street
Grimsby, Ontario
Tel: 905-945-5292
Fax: 905-945-0715
www.town.grimsby.on.ca
The museum is the place to start if you want to get a glimpse of Grimsby's fascinating past. Here you can see a scale model of the once magnificent round Methodist Campground Temple, modelled after the Morman Tabernacle in Utah. The original temple was made from laminated oak planks, with a dome that rose 31 metres (102 feet) above the floor. There were no interior pillars or supports that would obstruct the view or break up the seating area. It was here that 7,000 worshippers met for ten days every summer to pray and enjoy the fellowship of other families coming from isolated farms all over Ontario.

RECOMMENDED PRODUCERS

Puddicombe Estate Winery
J.B. Puddicombe & Sons
1468 Highway 8
Winona, Ontario, L8E 5K9
Tel: 905-643-1015
Fax: 905-643-0938
info@puddicombefarms.com

The evolution of the old No. 8 continued to echo the history of the region it traversed. By 1970, when the pressures of urban development became too serious for local governments throughout Niagara to control, government reform resulted in the amalgamation of Niagara's twelve municipalities into a regional government. This was when the No. 8 Highway became Regional 81, its present incarnation. To the natives, however, it's still the old No. 8 Highway.

Grimsby is the first major town along Regional Highway 81. The regal homes that line the highway as it passes through the heart of the old residential area are an elegant testimony to the agricultural prosperity of its early fruit farmers. The Niagara influence has defined Grimsby and its people since its early days, despite the fact that Grimsby is as close to Hamilton as it is to its sister towns in the Niagara Peninsula. Newcomers to Grimsby who work in Toronto and Hamilton are more likely to think along the Toronto-Hamilton axis rather than St. Catharines-Niagara, but in time, Niagara becomes the base of their identity.

Grimsby is a comfortable as well as convenient town. Although its population has tripled in size in the past few years, it is no stranger to large communities of people. Long before the first European "discovered" Niagara, there were upwards of 35,000 people living between Niagara-on-the-Lake and Grimsby — longtime residents of 2000 years ago. They were the Neutral Indians, a settled, Iroquois-speaking tribe, whose cultural artifacts have been unearthed by the plows of farmers in the region from its earliest days of settlement.

Flints, trail markers, mortars, pots and the remains of longhouses were brought to the surface as farmers cleared and tilled the land or as creek beds wore away the shore, revealing buried shards. But the most spectacular discoveries have been the Aboriginal burial grounds.

In October of 1976, a Grimsby builder discovered an assortment of iron axes, copper kettles and beads. He thought he had found relics from an old pioneer homestead until he uncovered some bones and a human skull. At that point he carefully covered his find and called the Royal Ontario Museum in Toronto.

It turned out to be a prehistoric find of major proportions. Major gaps in the history of these ancient peoples were filled. The Neutrals, or Attiwandarons, were a hospitable people, agricultural, tall and tattooed, who took a neutral stance between the warring Senecas and Hurons. They were skilled artisans who supplied flints made of limestone from the outcrops of the Escarpment. Their flint trade extended to tribes all over northeast America.

The legacy of the Neutrals remains steadfast. It is the Neutral name Ongniaahra (spellings vary) from which the name Niagara is derived. The memorial to their ossuary is at Centennial Park in the heart of Grimsby.

Intact are several nineteenth-century homes of architectural note. Of particular interest is Maplehurst (c. 1880) at 354 Main Street West. This Queen Anne-style home was built by the well-known editor and journalist, Linus Woolverton. His horticultural journal was one of the most well-read journals of its time. Woolverton was the first in the area to establish an experimental fruit station.

Farther along, at 271 Main Street West, is the Stone Shop, originally built as a blacksmith shop in the early 1800s. During the War of 1812 it was used by the troops — Canadian, British and American. Today it houses an art studio.

Another point of interest are the murals in the downtown area painted by a group of high school students.

PUDDICOMBE ESTATE

Puddicombe Estate is the first winery on the Highway #81 to launch the Niagara Wine along the Escarpment side of Niagara. The winery is only one piece of this multi-faceted farm experience. The Puddicombe farm has been in the family since 1797, so it is no wonder that they have a "family" view of hospitality. There is something for everyone, from premium wines made

View of Puddicombe's south escarpment

Puddicombe Estate

Daniel Lenko Estate Winery
Daniel Lenko Estate Winery
5246 Regional Road 81 [Old Number 8]
Beamsville, Ontario, L0R 1B3
Tel: 905-563-7756
Fax: 905-563-3317
Email: oldvines@DanielLenko.com
www.daniellenko.com
The Lenko family has been growing grapes for 40 years. As a matter of fact, their highly sought after Chardonnay and Merlot vines are the oldest in Ontario, producing fruit with rich, concentrated flavours that have been beautifully shepherded into wine by veteran winemaker, Jim Warren. One of Canada's most highly regarded winemakers, Warren had been using Lenko fruit for several years when he was at Stoney Ridge Cellars. It was natural for Warren to join the Lenkos when they decided to make wine as well.

Mom and Dad Lenko are still very much a part of the farm and winery, but son Daniel has taken over the day-to-day operation. The wines they produce are some of the finest in Canada — solid Chardonnays, tantalizing Viogniers, benchmark Gewurztraminers, velvety Merlots, Cabernets and Cabernet blends. Call ahead for an appointment. This is a working farm and Dan will probably have to hop off the tractor to greet you. The wines are only available at the winery.

Kittling Ridge Winery

ACCOMMODATIONS

Kittling Ridge Winery Inn and Suites
Windward Street
Grimsby, Ontario
Tel: 905-309-7171 or 1-800-446-5746
www.kittlingridge.com
Located across the QEW from the Kittling
Ridge Winery on Windward Road (accessed
by Casablanca Exit), the hotel-sized inn is
devoted to wine and includes all the amenities. Expansive Ontario wine list plus culinary
seminars on Niagara cuisine

RECOMMENDED PRODUCERS

**Kittling Ridge Estate Winery &
Spirits**
297 South Service Road
Grimsby, Ontario, L3M 1Y6
Tel: 905-945-9225
Fax: 905-945-9225
E-mail: admin@KittlingRidge.com
www.kittlingridge.com
Annual Production: 90,000 cases
Kittling Ridge is Canada's only winery and
distillery. Two educations for the price of one:
learn how spirits are made, as well as wine.
Taste their long line of wines, whiskeys,
vodkas and brandies, particularly the
Icewine/brandy.

Denwycke House at Grimsby
203 Main Street East
Grimsby, Ontario, L3M 1P5
Tel: 905-945-2149
Fax: 905-945-6272

from the farm's grapes, to a train ride tour of the farm aboard *Little Pudd.*
Enjoy a dinner or light snack in the tea room and café, or take time to shop
in the General Store.

The café offers light lunches, soups, sandwiches, freshly baked meat
pies, quiches and lasagna. The tearoom serves an assortment of teas and
coffees and a very popular English afternoon tea with homemade desserts.
Their line of wines includes a French Colombard seldom found in Niagara
which is a nicely crafted light-bodied white. Other wines to try are
Chardonnay, Viognier, Cabernet Franc and Gamay Noir.

Farther down the South Service Road is Grimsby's second winery and
Ontario's third largest, Kittling Ridge, named after the ridge of the
Escarpment above which, in the spring, migrating eagles, harriers, vultures,
falcons and hawks catch free rides on the invisible thermals that rise between
the Escarpment and the Lake. These majestic birds catch their breaths,
many coming from as far away as Brazil, before the next leg of their 1000-
mile flight to summer nesting grounds in the Arctic.

For a spectacular view of the Niagara Peninsula, follow the signs to
Beamer Point Conservation Area which has several observation platforms
deep within the Escarpment. Here you'll see what the birds see — a magnificent long, panoramic view of the Escarpment as it winds its way through
Niagara. Hundreds of bird lovers make Beamer Point their weekend
pilgrimage from March to May to watch and record up to 20,000 migrants.

From this vantage point you begin to appreciate the significant role the
Escarpment and the Lake play in this portion of Niagara's wine country.

Denwycke House at Grimsby

Insistent southwesterly winds from the lake are buffeted to shore when they reach the cliffs. This circulation system keeps warmer air circulating back over the land in fall, extending the growing season, and disturbs cold pockets in spring.

Across the QEW on Windward Road (accessed by Casablanca Exit), is the Kittling Ridge Winery Inn, a hotel-sized inn devoted to wine, from limo tours through wine country, to a pickup service for boaters who land at the Fifty Point Marina. What's fun here is the fact that you can sample Ontario's wines from the inn's expansive wine list in the eighth-floor lounge overlooking the lake, or have a culinary seminar on Niagara cuisine.

BEAMSVILLE

KITTLING RIDGE LTD.

Before John Hall bought the property which is now Kittling Ridge Winery and Distillery, it was the Rieder Distillery, built in 1971 by the Swiss still-master, Otto Rieder. Rieder produced fruit spirits (*eaux de vie* or fruit brandies) and soon expanded to include the more popular Canadian distilled spirits of vodka, whisky and grape brandy. In 1992, when Otto Rieder retired, John Hall assumed the position of CEO and took an equity position. In 1993 the distillery was granted a commercial winery license, making it the only combination winery and distillery operating in Ontario. The name was then changed to Kittling Ridge.

Email: johnpathunter@cs.com
www.denwycke.com
Built in 1846, the Denwycke (pronounced Den-wick) House bed and breakfast is a designated heritage home. The house's Georgian style with deep bracketed eaves is enhanced by ivy, which covers its solid brick walls. The home is furnished circa 1850 with Canadian and English antiques. It is centrally air-conditioned and the suites offer king-sized beds, attached private sitting rooms and ensuite, four-piece bathrooms. Hosts Patricia and John Hunter have been in the business for 15 years and understand what service and comfort means to a traveler. The gardens contain old Black Locust trees with deeply etched bark. The pioneers referred to the Black Locust as the "Nail Tree" explain the Hunters, because it made excellent pegs to hold together beams in early homes and barns. Rates: $95 - $110 single; $115-$130 double occupancy.

PLACES OF INTEREST

Beamer Memorial Conservation Area

Niagara Peninsula Conservation Authority
250 Thorold Road West, 3rd Floor
Welland, Ontario, L3C 3W2
Tel: 905-788-3135
www.conservation-niagara.on.ca
The 93-metre (305-foot) drop is sheer once you get there, so be careful. But it's worth the walk to observe the length of the Escarpment in Niagara. Here's your best chance to discover some of the unique flora and fauna that is characteristic of this majestic site.

FESTIVALS AND EVENTS

Hawkwatch at Beamer Memorial Conservation Area

Tel: 905-682-2090
www.freenet.hamilton.com.ca
Throughout weekends during March and April members of the Niagara Peninsula Hawkwatch will be on hand to help spot and identify hawks migrating north for the summer months. Wheelchair access, nature trail, water falls, majestic view.

BEAMSVILLE

RECOMMENDED PRODUCERS

Magnotta

4701 Ontario Street
Beamsville, Ontario, L0R 1B4
Tel: 905-563-5313
Fax: 905-563-8804
E-mail: magnotta@globalserve.net
www.magnotta.com
Annual Production: 250,000 cases
One of the very few wineries in Ontario to
sell wines predominantly through their own
five locations rather than the LCBO. Try their
sparkling Icewine and award-winning
Chardonnays. Fine retail shop.

Peninsula Ridge Estates

5600 King Street
Beamsville, Ontario, L0R 1B0
Tel: 905-563-0900
Fax: 905-563-0995
E-mail: prewl@vaxxine.com
www.peninsularidge.com
History and hospitality. On the walls of the
wine caves are medieval murals painted by
local artist Brian Romagnoli. Renowned
French winemaker Jean-Pierre Colas makes
their premium Chardonnay and Bordeaux-
style wines.

RESTAURANTS

The Restaurant at Peninsula Ridge

Tel: 905-563-0900 ext 35
www.peninsularidge.com/restaurant.html
The philosophy of cooking is based on clas-
sical French techniques but the cuisine is
rooted in Niagara. The restaurant uses ingredients from neighboring farms and orchards,
plus incorporating specialty products that
highlight the best of what Canada has to
offer, such as Quebec farmhouse cheeses,
and British Columbia and Maritime seafood.
Outdoor patio dining. Open Tuesday –
Sunday; lunch and dinner

During the next six years John Hall built the business into the sixth largest winery in Ontario, and his Pure Gold Whisky became the third most popular imported spirit in Taiwan. In 1997 the company launched Inferno Pepper Pot Vodka, which was soon followed by Forty Creek Whisky, and a series of Maple-based products that provided a Canadian touch to their product repertoire. Today Kittling Ridge has expanded and is now producing 100,000 cases of wine and spirits a year. It is an interesting place to stop and tour, especially to view the great copper pot still and the column still in their distillery. Also it's a treat to try some of their fine whiskies and brandies.

Beamsville can be reached by either continuing east on Regional Highway 81 from Grimsby or by exiting the QEW at the first Beamsvlle exit. Continue south until you reach Regional Highway 81 — the Niagara Wine Route.

With the government reform that resulted in the amalgamation of several communities in Niagara (1970), the Town of Lincoln was formed by joining the villages of Beamsville, Vineland, Jordan and Campden. Other communities throughout the peninsula were similarly consolidated into municipalities such as St. Catharines, Niagara-on-the-Lake, Welland, Port Colborne and Fort Erie. Because politics and economies of scale ruled over community identity and affiliation, communities in Niagara still bicker, vying for sovereignty and autonomy, reinforcing the persistent tide lines of smaller community identity, much to the chagrin of local politicians. A person from Beamsville does not blur the difference between him or her and a person from Vineland, even though the neighbouring village might be just a farm away, and they are both technically from the Town of Lincoln.

Beamsville, home of the first hockey net, the first commercial peach orchard in Canada and the first commercially made cheese, dates back to the late 1700s when Jacob Beam first cleared his Crown lands to farm. Beam, a Loyalist, had been jailed in the U.S. for harbouring British soldiers. His land had been confiscated, but so determined was he to start life over in Upper Canada he transported his entire family through dense forests and rough trails. In their covered wagon, "packed to the boards" with furniture, utensils, warm clothes and tools, he included a mill saw and his bolting cloth. He also included his notebook of records of purchase of 410 pounds of iron for the mill he was going to build.

William Kitchen settled in a nearby farm and by 1790 Kitchen and Beam joined forces to build a grist and sawmill on Kitchen's farm. The long, one-storey mill stood just below the Escarpment's ridge. This Beam-Kitchen enterprise formed the hub around which a busy community grew.

By the mid-1800s, Kitchen had also planted grapes on his farm from

Left: *Peninsula Ridge*

Edgewater Manor
518 Fruitland Road
Stoney Creek, Ontario, L8E 5A6
Tel: 905-643-9332
Fax: 905-643-8477
Overlooking Lake Ontario, the mansion was built in 1922 by a prominent lawyer, P.R. Morris, whose dream was to build his own private castle as a testament to his success. The crash of '29 ended his dream, but his son fulfilled it 20 years later. New owners converted the family home into fine dining.

Angel Food Café
45 Ontario Street
Grimsby, Ontario,
Tel: 905-945-5522
A couple of doors away from Fork Road Pottery is this delightfully renovated nineteenth-century home with an eclectic menu featuring an all-Ontario wine list. Alfresco dining in the summer in their expansive courtyard is a treat. In between is heritage mill, the brainchild of cabinetmaker George Oost, who renovated the turn-of-the-century basket factory that now houses specialty shops.

FESTIVALS AND EVENTS

Festival of The Forty
Tel: 905-945-8319
www.jefs.com/forty
Held annually the third week in August, with midway rides and games, video, dance, dancers, a quilting bee, bands, theatre, contests and parade — good old-fashioned summer fun. Held in Coronation Park.

The Strawberry Festival
Tel: 905-563-7403
www.townoflincoln.com
Held in downtown Beamsville the third week in June. A day of old-fashioned sidewalk sales, strawberry shortcake and entertainment.

which he made wine from native grapes, and produced enough to advertise his products. Kitchen's broadsheet declared that his wines were "in use by some Hundreds of churches for sacramental services" and were "in the principal drug stores in Canada East and West." (By the mid-1800s Upper Canada and Lower Canada were changed to Canada East and West. With Confederation in 1867, they became known as Ontario and Quebec.)

This is the western branch of the Beamsville Bench, the step-like ridge of prime land that parallels the Escarpment and the beginning of the most dramatic vineyards in Niagara. Although Lake Ontario exercises a moderating influence over all of the Niagara Peninsula, the regional mesoclimate is far from homogeneous. Just below the cliffs of the Escarpment the bench of tiered slopes gives rise to air flows with different rates of warming and cooling from the rest of the peninsula. The Escarpment acts as a shelter against which the prevailing winds off the lake are circulated back to shore, creating a well-drained and protected zone. New vineyard and winery development here has exceeded any other part of Ontario.

PENINSULA RIDGE

Jacob Beam gave his name to the town. The Kitchen legacy lives on, however, at Peninsula Ridge Estates Winery, located on the same site as the original Beam-Kitchen mill. Although the mill is gone, the 1885 home of Kitchen's grandson is now a fine-dining restaurant. This exquisite 80-acre property sits on the prime land of the Beamsville Bench. Here proprietor

EastDell Estates Winery
4041 Locust Lane
Beamsville, Ontario, L0R 1B0
Tel: 905-563-9463
Fax: 905-563-4633
www.eastdell.com
The winery restaurant of EastDell Estates is located on 62 acres of vineyards, ponds, wooded hiking trails and a magnificent hilltop view of Lake Ontario and the Toronto skyline. Great spot for Sunday brunch, lunch or dinner. Wines are food friendly. Moderate prices.

Thirty Bench Vineyard and Winery
4281 Mountainview Road
Beamsville, Ontario, L0R 1B0
Tel: 905-563-1698
Fax: 905-563-3921
E-mail: wine@thirtybench.com
www.thirtybench.com
Annual Production: 10,000 cases
Located near the Thirty Mile Creek, Thirty Bench is for the wine enthusiast with a cellar or one who wants to start. These wines are built for the long haul. Go to taste wines. No bells and whistles, just superb Cabernets, Chardonnays and Rieslings.

Norm Beal has planted 60 acres of vinifera varieties including Cabernet Sauvignon, Cabernet Franc, Merlot, Chardonnay, Sauvignon Blanc, Viognier and Syrah. Jean-Pierre Colas came to Peninsula Ridge after a decade of distinction as head winemaker at Domain Laroche in Chablis, France. Colas' intention, however, is not to make French wines in Canada, but rather to discover the particular personality of the fruit grown in Niagara and to guide that character into the bottle. A master with Chardonnay, his are robust, yet refined with a backbone of acidity that stands up well to food. His Sauvignon Blanc is one of the finest in Canada. His reds display a depth and integration that points to equally fine results as they mature. Most exciting in the Colas lineup is his Syrah. Who would have thought this delight of the northern Rhone could show such depth and white peppery varietal character in Ontario?

The retail shop is located in a restored post and beam barn, built in 1885, where you can taste wines and have a guided tour through their modern facilities.

The wines are just one jewel in the Peninsula Ridge crown. The property features a landmark home, the 1885 Queen Anne revival manor, once the residence of Kitchen's grandson. The distinctive design includes a magnificent turret and cedar-shingled roof. The home, which sits high on a knoll in the middle of the vineyard, has been carefully restored and is now one of Ontario's finest restaurants.

All along the Regional Highway 81, pristine Victorian homes still line the Escarpment ridge. Visit the Tea Room at the bottom of Thirty Road or Walker Hall, on the lakeside of Grimsby at the bottom of Mountainview Road.

EastDell Estates Winery

De Sousa Wine Cellars
3753 Quarry Rd.
Beamsville, Ontario, L0R 1B0
Tel: 905-563-7269
Fax: 905-563-9404
Email: desousa@desousawinery.com
www.desousawines.com
Toronto Location:
802 Dundas Street West
Toronto, Ontario, M6J 1U3
Tel: 416-603-0202
Fax: 905-338-9404

The De Sousa family chose the vineyards of Niagara to make wines in the Portuguese tradition. All their reds are aged in oak to achieve flavours that most closely resemble wines made in the Portuguese tradition. Unique to De Sousa Wine Cellars is the tradition of tasting wine in a clay cup. Says John De Sousa, "Many a skeptic has become a believer!" In the spring of 1998 they opened their Toronto facility — the only winery located in the heart of Toronto. The Beamsville location is a delightful, two-storey, white frame structure with wrought iron window balconies, and an adjoining tasting room and retail operation. Most of their wines are VQA products and all are under $15. These include Cabernet Sauvignon, Cabernet Franc, Marechal Foch, Baco Noir, Chardonnay and Riesling, plus a non-VQA port and port reserve.

The architectural jewel in Beamsville is the Regency Woodburn Cottage and Tearoom (1834), on Highway 81 now a bed and breakfast with beautiful gardens and a completely refurbished, but authentic interior.

Trinity United Church on William Street has extremely rare stained glass windows designed by McCausland of Toronto. Worth seeing.

THIRTY BENCH VINEYARD AND WINERY

Just off Regional Highway 81 on Mountainview Road is Thirty Bench, best known for their handcrafted and long-lived wines. Theirs is a unique team of three semi-independent managing partner/winemakers, each responsible for a different part of the winemaking agenda. Dr. Tom Muckle, a physician, is responsible for the Rieslings; Frank Zeritsch, a Hamilton businessman, makes the Icewine and a Vidal-Riesling blend, and Yorgos Papageorgiou, a McMaster professor, is responsible for their barrel-room Cabernets, Merlots and Chardonnays. They grow their grapes differently from most — close to the ground with a bigger canopy.

EASTDELL ESTATES WINERY

Continue south on Mountainview and left/east on Locust Lane and you arrive at the 50 acre estate of EastDell Estates founded in 1999 by Susan O'Dell and Michael East. EastDell produces a variety of wines including a specialty range of fruit wines.

The symbol found on all EastDell wine is the Blue Heron. Adopted as the

Silver Birches By The Lake

ACCOMMODATIONS
Silver Birches By The Lake
4902 Mountainview Road
Beamsville, Ontario, L0R 1B3
Tel/Fax: 905-563-9479
Email: info@SilverBirchesByTheLake.com
www.silverbirchesbythelake.com
Just a short walk to the lake, this lovely Bed
and Breakfast is located in the fruitlands of
Beamsville. It has a terrific pool and a great
tennis court. The tiered deck with pond and
waterfall in the back is an ideal place to
unwind or watch the sunset. They also have
bicycles that guests can use to tour the area.
There is a boat ramp nearby which provides
access to Lake Ontario for water sports and
fishing. A four-course dinner is available if
booked in advance. Rates: $105 double
occupancy.

Thomas and Vaughan Vintners
4245 King Street
Beamsville, Ontario, L0R 1B1
Tel: 905-563-7737
Fax: 905-563-4114
www.thomasandvaughan.com
Annual Production: 4,000 cases
Located directly on Highway 81, grape
grower Tom Kocsis and his wife, Barbara
Vaughan, decided to make their own wine
from their grapes — the same grapes so
many others had been using to win awards.
Try their old vines Chardonnay, Pinot Gris
and Icewine.

Angels Gate Winery

company's logo, the heron represents the beauty of the nature found along
the famed biosphere of the Niagara Escarpment. This site, in particular, has
one of the most commanding views of the Escarpment and Lake Ontario.

Extensive mapping was done to determine local flora and fauna along
a system of Escarpment trails surrounding the property. The winery also
features an on-site restaurant, The Bench Bistro with seasonal menus
focusing on regional cuisine. Prices are moderate. View outstanding.

ANGELS GATE WINERY
Across the road from Thirty Bench is one of Niagara's newest wineries.
Established in June 2002, Angels Gate is a dream come true for entrepreneurs and amateur winemakers Catherine and Dave Burr. The property is
magnificent. It is lovingly landscaped, with thousands of indigenous
flowers along a gently cascading spring, and the Niagara Escarpment and
Bruce Trail as a backdrop. The foreground is their vineyard and a spectacular view of the peninsula and the Toronto skyline.

The winery has been constructed underground with two naturally cooled barrel cellars and an observation gallery above the cellar floor. Upstairs, the tasting room and retail shop co-exist in a spacious room, opened to the countryside by enormous arching windows that frame the magnificent scenery. Not to be missed is the view from their three-storey tower where you can spot Buffalo, Niagara Falls, the mouth of the Welland Canal and Toronto. Light fare is available on an outdoor patio .

They produce Chardonnay, Vidal Blanc, a killer Pinot Noir, Cabernet Sauvignon, Cabernet Franc, Zweigelt, Merlot, and Gewurztraminer. The Burrs were so passionate about wine, they sold their two home wine making supply stores in Cambridge and Guelph, and bought this stunning 26-acre property that was once a mission for a convent. That, combined with the fact that the Burrs felt that the property was heaven on earth, led to the name Angels Gate. It is a tranquil place in the country where you can take your time sipping, strolling, hiking, nibbling, smelling…

The Malivoire Wine Company

Directly on Highway 81 but tucked at the top of the slope. Special effects film producer, Martin Malivoire, has stretched a Quonset Hut down an Escarpment hillside and transformed it into an ingenious five-storey winery, converting it from warehouse bleak to Bauhaus sleek. The hill, inhospitable to grapes, was a perfect place to build a gravity-driven operation.

There are two mezzanines on which winemaking tanks and other equipment are located and that intersect three stairlike levels. As one process is finished, the wine is gently siphoned down to the next process. The grapes they learned would grow best on the site are Gewurztraminer, Chardonnay, Chardonnay Musqué, Gamay Noir, Pinot Noir, and Pinot Gris. They use no pesticides or herbicides, wooden posts in the vineyard rather than steel, and they harvest by hand rather than machine. They welcome visitors, but request a phone call before you arrive.

For another Niagara Escarpment experience visit **Crown Bench**, tucked deep inside the Escarpment (south on Aberdeen) atop the ridge and beside a stream. Crown Bench is owned by Peter Kocsis and specializes in creamy Chardonnays.

Along Regional Highway 81, just east of the Malivoire Wine Company is **Thomas and Vaughan Vintners**. Famous husband and wife team Tom Kocsis (cousin of Peter Kocsis, Crown Bench) and Barbara Vaughan turned their vineyard into a winery when they saw that everyone else was winning awards with the quality of their fruit. Small, but quite attentive.

RECOMMENDED PRODUCERS

Angels Gate Winery
4260 Mountainview Road
Beamsville, Ontario, L0R 1B2
Tel: 905-563-3942
Fax: 905-563-4127
www.angelsgatewinery.com

Angels Gate Winery

The Malivoire Wine Company
P.O. Box 475
4260 King Street
Beamsville, Ontario, L0R 1B0
Tel: 905-563-9253
Fax: 905-563-9512
E-mail: ladybug@malivoirewineco.com
www.malivoirewineco.com
Annual production: 4,000 cases
Respect for the environment and a focus on the vineyard combined with a non-interventionist approach in the cellar results in some of the most eloquent wines in the Peninsula. Look for their talisman: the ladybug.

Crown Bench Estates
3850 Aberdeen Road
Beamsville, Ontario, L0R 2B6
Tel: 905-563-3959
Fax: 905-563-3441
www.crownbenchestates.com
Vineyard guided tours and tastings with raconteur/proprietor/winemaker Peter Kocsis. Naturalist tours and herbal tea weekends. Entrance to the Bruce Trail. Beautiful site nestled in embrace of the Escarpment.

THE TWENTY MILE VALLEY: VINELAND

Between Vineland and Jordan lies the corridor of the Twenty Mile Creek, the largest creek in the Niagara watershed. Its waters flow through some of the most varied landscapes in Ontario and at one point transforms itself into a spectacular falls (Balls Falls) as it meets the rocky dome of the Niagara Escarpment. From there it winds its way serenely into the safety of Jordan Harbour before joining Lake Ontario. Along its banks early settlers built their homesteads and towns were formed around its trading, milling and transportation crossroads.

Because of its many unique features, Twenty Mile Creek is recognized as an Environmentally Significant Area with Biological Sensitivity of unusual plants, wildlife, landforms and breeding grounds. There are thirteen nationally or provincially rare species and a high concentration of species (forty-one) that are only found in the Carolinian Zone of which this is a part.

Of the fauna, there are eleven rare or endangered species including the Eastern Blackbird, the Pickerel Frog, the Eastern Spring Soft-shelled Turtle and the Green Sunfish.

The valley of the Twenty Mile Creek is also an apt illustration of the fickle manner in which centres live or die. Rockway Falls, for instance, was once a bustling salt springs. Today it is marked by a community centre and a cemetery. Jordan Harbour, once a thriving port that shipped wheat and tender fruit to Montreal and Great Britain, is gone. Only a small marina

Left: *Jordan Harbour*   Top: *Balls Falls*

PLACES OF INTEREST

Balls Falls and Conservation Area

From QEW Niagara take Exit 57 (Victoria Avenue) in Vineland and travel south to the entrance of Balls Falls on your left.

This popular Escarpment conservation area features the scenic natural beauty of two cataracts and heritage buildings forming a pioneer village reminiscent of this once-industrial mid-nineteenth-century hamlet. Visitors enjoy tours of the heritage buildings, hikes along the nature trails, special workshops and events.

For more information contact:
Niagara Peninsula Conservation Authority
250 Thorold Road West (3rd floor)
Welland, Ontario, L3C 3W2
Tel: 905-788-3135
www.conservation-niagara.on.ca

Niagara Under Glass Discovery Centre

1 Discovery Lane, P.O. Box 10
Vineland, Ontario, L0R 2C0
Tel: 905-562-4400
Fax: 905-562-4393
Email: info@niagaraunderglass.com
www.niagaraunderglass.com

Balls Falls heritage building

testifies to its vibrant past. Tintern, the birthplace of Governor General Roland Michener, consists of a church and a sign.

Glen Elgin had the most illustrious past of all as a thriving milling community, with the promise of becoming a prominent city centre, but it too was forsaken, although not forgotten.

The Balls Falls Conservation Centre is now a restored pioneer village in a scenic setting reliving life as it was once lived through a number of nineteenth-century buildings including a grist mill, log cabins, a blacksmith shop, a church, the old Ball family home, a lime kiln and an apple-drying shed. Yet other settlements of the Twenty prevailed.

Vineland and Jordan are rewarded today for their persistence with a vitality prompted by the thriving wine industry surrounding the valley. Vineland, always an agricultural hamlet, grew around Moyer's General Store at the corner of the old Queenston and Grimsby Stone Road (Regional Highway 81) and Victoria Avenue, the only approach up the hill to the mills at Balls Falls.

Of interest to gardeners is the Vineland Horticultural Station, now part of the University of Guelph. The gardens are restful. Further along towards the lake is the Millennium Forest, an area devoted to indigenous flora. It's marked by a community plaque.

The first people to settle in the area were soldiers who had served with the illustrious Butler's Rangers, along with civilian United Empire Loyalists who were given land grants as a reward for their loyalty to the British Crown during the American Revolutionary War. They were joined in 1799 by another group of Loyalists, Pennsylvania German Mennonites, seeking a refuge in which to worship free from the harassment of patriotic Americans. They bought 1,100 acres of land from the Loyalists who were beginning to clear the land there.

So began the Twenty Mile Valley — its early pioneers a strange and paradoxical mixture of political conviction and religious ardour, soldiers who bore arms and worshippers who were adamant in their refusal to do so. Yet their courage coalesced to forge industry out of the wilderness. That determination united them and the fertile Valley of the Twenty rewarded them.

Among the first group of Pennsylvania German Mennonite settlers were the High family. A fine example of Mennonite architecture can be found on Victoria Avenue off South at the intersection of Regional Highway 81 and Victoria Avenue. on the top of the Escarpment. It is called Chestnut Hall, the home and antique shop of Mr. Barclay Holmes. It is a sturdy red-brick, two-storey home built by Daniel High in 1837, with a side addition called a "daughty house" for the parents.

The Niagara Under Glass Discovery Centre is a 15,000 sq. ft. facility where you can learn how greenhouses work: how technology works with plants to purify air and water; how a green house operates, illustrated through a working scale-model greenhouse; how plants grow indoors using hydroponics. An elevated walkway provides a view of the potted plant production area, alive with calla lilies, miniature roses and chrysanthemums. Children and adults can take a twenty-minute potting class or learn how to grow plants from cuttings. Once completely packaged, visitors can take their plants home. Open 10 – 4 Monday-Saturday, $5 adults; $2.50 children, wheelchair friendly.

FESTIVALS AND EVENTS

Steve Bauer Bike Tours
P.O. Box 428
Vineland, Ontario, L0R 2C0
Tel: 905-562-0788
Fax: 905-562-0674
E-mail: bike@SteveBauer.com
www.stevebauer.com/contact
Take a bike tour through Jordan and Balls Falls in and out of the Escarpment. Lunch at Vineland Estates, visiting other wineries along the way. Also available for touring in Niagara-on-the-Lake.

Niagara Nature, Wine and Garden Tours
R.R. #1
Vineland Station, Ontario, L0R 2E0
Tel: 905-562-3746
E-mail: nnt@vaxxine.com
www.niagaranaturetours.com
Join a qualified naturalist in nature outings through wine country. Learn about some of Niagara's rare species of plants and animals and folklore.

RESTAURANTS

Vineland Estates Restaurant
R. R. #1
3620 Moyer Road
Vineland, Ontario, L0R 2C0
Tel: 905-562-7088
Fax: 905-562-3071
www.vineland.com/dinersguide.html
Located on the Vineland Estates winery property in the original 1840s homestead, since renovated yet retaining its historic charm. Listed in En Route's Top 100 Restaurants in Canada. Inventive seasonal menus based on locally sourced, fresh products. Picturesque and lovely.

RECOMMENDED PRODUCERS

Vineland Estates Wines, Ltd.
R.R. #1
3620 Moyer Road
Vineland, Ontario, L0R 2C0
Tel: 905-562-7088
Fax: 905-562-3071
E-mail: wine@vineland.com
www.vineland.com
Annual Production: 35,000 cases
This property has it all — beauty, fine dining, classy retail shop and fine wines. A visit to Niagara would be incomplete without it. Lunch or dinner on the winedeck is a moment to remember.

VINELAND ESTATES

Nearly 150 years later, and just a couple of kilometres away, another German, Herman Weis, also saw the potential that lay in the rolling Vineland hills. In 1979, Weis bought an old farmhouse (c.1840) and farm and planted 45 acres of his special Riesling clone (21B), then named the vineyard St. Urban's after the vineyard of the same name on his Mosel Valley estate.

When the vines started to bear fruit he built a winery and called it Vineland Estates. In 1992 entrepreneur John Howard bought the winery, increased the area under vine to 275 acres and developed it into one of Canada's benchmark operations. Particularly outstanding is the winery restaurant, opened in 1995 that showcases Vineland Estates wines and Niagara-based cuisine. Vineland Estates is known for their rich Chardonnays, long-lived Cabernets and Merlots and their signature wines — very fine Rieslings made in every style from dry to Icewine as well as a Riesling-based sparkling. Among their many amenities (a carriage house for private functions, a fully-stocked retail store, winedeck dining), they have a helicopter landing pad for those afternoons when the traffic is just too much to abide!

FEATHERSTONE ESTATE WINERY AND VINEYARD

Further up Victoria Avenue, just past Moyer Road is the entrance to Featherstone, which is marked by a massive rock carved by local artisan Jim Scott. The commissioned piece called *Carved in Stone*, is an engraved seven ton chunk of pink Peterborough granite. The winery name is carved beside a large feather, which, paradoxically, appears to be fossilized. Featherstone Estate Winery is among the newcomers to the region, owned and operated

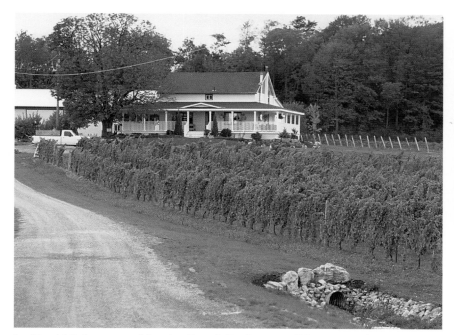

Featherstone Estate Winery and Vineyard
3678 Victoria Avenue
Vineland, Ontario, L0R 2C0
Tel: 905-562-1949
Fax: 905-562-3989
Email: featherstonewinery@sympatico.ca

Lakeview Cellars Estate Winery, Ltd.
R.R. #1, 4037 Cherry Avenue
Vineland, Ontario, L0R 2C0
Tel: 905-562-5685
Fax: 905-562-0673
E-mail: icew@vaxxine.com
www.lakeviewcellars.on.ca
Annual production: 11,000 cases
Pretty Beamsville Bench site. Expanded tasting room and retail shop. Best noted for big reds (Baco Noir, Cabernets.) Age-worthy wines with a proven track record.

by David Johnson and Louise Engel. Both are well known and respected in the Guelph area for their famous Guelph Poultry Gourmet Market, which they established in 1986. As successful as they were, David couldn't resist the lure of farming and wine making. With his first commercial vintage he won an award at the March 2002 Winemakers' Selection Competition. The farm's rolling hills provide a bucolic setting for visitors.

Wines include Riesling, Chardonnay and Cabernet Franc, all produced in small lots for greater control. The tasting room is housed in a portion of the 1830s farmhouse, where you can taste David's handcrafted, very well made wines.

LAKEVIEW CELLARS

Around the corner from Vineland Estates, on Cherry Avenue is Lakeview Cellars, a medium-sized winery set on the Beamsville Bench that specializes in robust red wines and fruity whites.

In 1986, award-winning amateur winemaker Eddy Gurinksas retired from his Ottawa job with the railroad and bought a 13-acre vineyard with his wife, Lorraine. Their plan was to plant and nurture their own grapes for their own wines. Five years later, urged by their winemaking friends, Eddy and Lorraine founded Lakeview Cellars. As production grew, nearby grower Larry Hipple joined the partnership, soon followed by jet pilot Stu Morgan.

Eddy and Lorraine concentrate on making big, age-worthy Bordeaux-style reds, and Lakeview Cellars is one of only four other Ontario producers who make the aromatic, unoaked, Chardonnay Musqué. (The others are Malivoire, Vineland Estates and Cave Spring Cellars.)

BIRCHWOOD ESTATES WINERY

Birchwood Estates Winery is located at the foot of Cherry Avenue on the south service road, parallel to the QEW in Beamsville. It was established in May 2000, and is committed to producing quality wines at affordable prices. The vines are over fifteen years old and were planted by the original owners, Willow Heights, who were so successful they had to expand their operation to Regional Road 81.

This location's proximity to the lake keeps it cooler in spring when the danger of late frost could kill young buds, and warmer in fall and winter thanks to the lake's radiant warmth. Despite its short history, the winery has already received awards for its Gewurztraminer/Riesling.

WILLOW HEIGHTS

Driving north on Cherry Road to Regional Highway 81, turn right. A short distance away on your left you'll discover Willow Heights Estate — a hacienda-styled winery with stucco walls, ceramic floors, a red-tiled roof and pergola that shelters a patio as charming and classic as any found in the heart of Napa. This fine winery is owned and operated by the Speranzini family — Ron Speranzini is winemaker and his daughter Nicole manages the retail store. Speranzini originally came from the ranks of other successful amateur winemakers such as Jim Warren (formerly with Stoney Ridge Cellars), Eddy Gurinksas (Lakeview Cellars) and John Marynissen (Marynissen Estates). So good were his wines that the others encouraged him to make them commercially. Up until the late nineties he continued to work at Stelco as a quality assurance manager. Full-time now at the winery, his approach to quality continues.

KACABA VINEYARDS

Located on the slopes of the Escarpment near Vineland, Kacaba [Kah-sah-bah] Vineyards is directly on the Wine Route on Highway 81. A footbridge purchased from the St. Lawrence Seaway crosses a small terraced ravine, where owner Michael Kacaba first planted Syrah. Across the bridge is a planting of Cabernet Sauvignon, Cabernet Franc and Merlot. A cupola with a horse on its weather-vane commemorates the fact that the property

Birchwood Estates Winery
4679 Cherry Avenue
Vineland, Ontario, LOR 1B0
Tel: 905-562-6344
Fax: 905-562-8463
www.birchwoodwines.com

Willow Heights Estate Winery
R.R. #1
3751 Regional Road 81
Vineland, Ontario, LOR 2C0
Tel: 905-562-4945
Fax: 905-562-5761
E-mail: willow.heights@sympatico.com
www.willowheights.on.ca
Annual production: 10,000 cases
A hacienda in the heart of Niagara.
Outdoor patio with casual dining, live music
and very fine wines. A pleasant experience.

Kacaba Vineyards

Kacaba Vineyards

Kacaba Vineyards
3550 King Street
Vineland, Ontario
Tel: 905-562-5625
Email: staff@kacaba.com
www.kacaba.com

Stoney Ridge Cellars
3201 King Street
Vineland, Ontario, L0R 2C0
Tel: 905-562-1324
Fax: 905-562-7777
E-mail:srcellar@vaxxine.com
www.stoneyridgecellar.com
Annual production: 55,000 cases
Present location in transition, but the wines are
very fine indeed. Worth sampling are some
of his expanded line of fruit wines, sherries
and ports.

was once an active horse ranch.

Although a Bay Street lawyer today, Michael Kacaba is descended from grape growing and wine producing families in the Ukraine. He also grew up on a farm in western Canada, so building a winery was like coming home. The winery is a family operation run by his wife Joanne and their three daughters. Award-winning winemaker Jim Warren makes their wines, which are showcased in several leading Toronto restaurants. Their Chardonnays and Merlots are particularly popular. Besides restaurants, their wines are available only at the winery.

STONEY RIDGE CELLARS

A stone's throw away on Regional Highway 81 is the temporary home of Stoney Ridge Cellars, originally founded by Jim Warren, the winemaker responsible for establishing Stoney Ridge's reputation for producing very fine wines. Warren left the winery in May 2000, to consult and to lend his experience to the fledging Fruit Wine Association of Ontario. Proprietor John Belanger will no doubt continue the level of fine wines that Warren established.

Look for Warren's influence at Lenko Vineyards (Beamsville), the grape grower from whom Warren bought many of his grapes. Son Danny Lenko is now opening a winery of his own under Warren's winemaking tutelage.

The Twenty Mile Valley: Jordan

After winding and dipping your way through the undulating Jordan Valley, make a sharp left turn at the top of the road onto Main Street, Jordan. Take this road to the end and you'll be in the tiny hamlet of Jordan, adjacent to the Twenty Mile Creek and the home of Cave Spring Cellars winery. I like Jordan because its past is preserved in gentle ways without the patina and veneer that often accompanies towns that have been restored by eager contemporary developers. You won't get the feeling that the town is a movie set behind which Disney Studios store their cameras. Jordan is genuine.

Jordan got its name from the Pennsylvania German Mennonites who arrived in the late 1700s. After the long journey from Pennsylvania by Conestoga Wagon, they arrived in the Twenty Mile Valley area and felt they had "come home." The main street began to take shape in 1837 when Jacob Snure purchased land from Abraham High (father of Daniel High, whose 1837 home now houses Chestnut Hall on Victoria Avenue in Vineland) Snure, the entrepreneur, reasoned that farmers in the district needed a village to provide goods and services they couldn't provide for themselves. He surveyed the land and sold lots to tanners, masons, tailors, innkeepers, blacksmiths and harness-and-wagon makers. They, in turn, built and lived in the Georgian and Victorian homes that still line Main Street.

Left: *Wismer Farm, Jordan*   Top: *Local fruit and flower stand*

RECOMMENDED PRODUCERS

Cave Spring Cellars
3838 Main Street
P.O. Box 53
Jordan, Ontario, L0R 1S0
Tel: 905-562-3581
Fax: 905-562-3232
E-mail: bdettorr@cavespringcellars.com
www.cavespringcellars.com
Annual production: 60,000 cases
One of the oldest blocks of vinifera vines at
the Cave Spring vineyard in Beamsville, now
expanded to 100 acres of high density vineyards, including the first planting of Chenin
Blanc and Semillon in Niagara. The village
of Jordan is a pleasing destination with
shops, inns, Cave Spring Cellars winery and
tasting room and the famous On the Twenty
restaurant. Not to be missed!

Jordan prospered for many years, never exceeding its own definition as a centre devoted to serving the commercial needs of the agricultural community that surrounded it. The products shifted from wheat to apples and other tender fruit, then grapes, but the service remained the same. In the twenties a winery (Jordan-Ste. Michelle) located where the canning factory once stood produced some of Ontario's leading labels, but in the mid-eighties it closed its doors. This was the same time that a young university professor, Len Pennachetti, was looking for a facility where he and his family could make wine from the grapes they harvested from their young Beamsville vineyard. In 1978, they had been among the first to take the risk of planting a vineyard dedicated 100 percent to vinifera vines. (Many others in the region hedged their bets in the early days by planting French hybrids and a small percentage of vinifera.)

Pennachetti named the winery after the vineyard — Cave Spring Cellars. He jumped at the opportunity to buy the old Jordan-Ste. Michelle winery in 1986. The site at the time was empty and overgrown. The only

reason to visit Jordan was the Jordan Museum, whose collection was a great source of local history and a fine antique shop. That was it. But that wasn't what Pennachetti saw.

When Pennachetti bought the property, he, like Snure 150 years before him, saw the possibilities of serving a new constituent — the wine enthusiast. Besides his winery, Pennachetti saw antique shops, galleries, garden shops, restaurants, book stores and an inn of country comfort and city panache. Take a look at Jordan today and you'll understand the meaning of vision.

In 1993, Pennachetti and his partners opened On the Twenty, the first winery restaurant in Canada dedicated to promoting the best wine and food of Niagara. In 1996 they opened The Inn on the Twenty, the first full-service overnight accommodation at a winery, designed and managed by Pennachetti's wife, Helen Young. From the restaurant you can see the steep and quite beautiful Twenty Mile Valley. Along the creek side at the bottom of the valley floor are walking paths for exploration and enjoyment.

Through Pennachetti's leadership the drowsy town of Jordan was awakened to become a lovely destination, intricately and carefully integrated into the historic townscape. Jacob Snure would be proud.

Growers and entrepreneurs like Pennachetti were among the first to

Above: *On the Twenty Restaurant*
Below: *Vintner's Inn*

ACCOMMODATIONS

The Inn on the Twenty
3845 Main Street
Jordan, Ontario, L0R 1S0
Tel: 905-562-3581
Fax: 905-562-3232
E-mail: vintners@niagara.net
www.vintnersinn.on.ca
Located on the second and third storeys of a renovated nineteenth-century sugar warehouse. Sixteen elegant suites with living room, fireplace, bedroom, full bath. Across from On the Twenty and Cave Spring Cellars Winery in the heart of the historic village of Jordan. Meeting rooms. Rates: $199-$275.

Jordan's Main Street

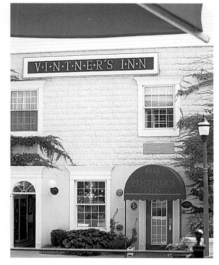

RECOMMENDED PRODUCERS

Harbour Estates Winery

4362 Jordan Road
Jordan Station, Ontario, L0R 1S0
Tel: 905-562-4639 or 1-877-HEW-WINE
Fax: 905-562-3839
www.hewwine.com
Beautiful site, 30 feet above Jordan Harbour.
Walking trails on a unique part of the Twenty
Mile Creek corridor. A nature lover's and
wine lover's dream.

PLACES OF INTEREST

Jordan Historical Museum of the Twenty

3802 Main Street
Jordan, Ontario, L0R 1S0
Tel: 905-562-5242
Fax: 905-562-7786
E-mail: jhmtchin@vaxxine.com
www.tourismniagara.com/jordanmuseum
Besides one of the finest collections of 200-
year-old fraktur art (a form of Latin lettering
used in German printing where colourful
motifs decorate documents and manuscripts)
the museum has two buildings of interest: an
old school house (1859) that displays one of
the most unusual pioneer collections of farm
implements in Ontario, and The Fry House, a
two-storey log cabin, once the home of Jacob
Fry, "a weaver of unusual merit," and the only
example of a pioneer home furnished with
original materials. The Fry House is located in
the old Mennonite Church cemetery and on
the tombstones is the mystery of Nancy High.
See if you can find it!

Jordan Village

Located on the green bank of the Twenty Mile
Creek, the village has intriguing shops on Main
Street including The Copper Leaf Garden
Store, which contains hard-to-find plants and
gorgeous garden accessories; Jordan Antiques
Centre — twenty-five professional dealers in
7,000 sq. ft.; Tintern-on-Main with designer
clothing and accessories; Ninavik Gallery —
native arts; The Art Vine and Books Store with
top-of-the line wine and art books.

View of Twenty Mile Valley

take the risk to plant the better quality vinifera grapes. Their risk paved the way for others to follow, not the least of whom is a new player in the Jordan area — the Boisset firm from France, one of the largest producers in Burgundy. In a joint venture with Vincor, Canada's largest wine company and the fourth-largest winery in North America, they've purchased seventy-seven acres of Bench slopes in Jordan and named it Le Clos Jordan. Here they plan to produce Pinot Noir and Chardonnay. The world-renowned architect Frank Gehry is designing the winery. For now, the wines will be made at the Jackson-Triggs Winery in Niagara-on-the-Lake, a sister winery.

Leaving Cave Spring Cellars, turn left on 19th Street, then a quick right onto Fourth Avenue. There are three wineries on this part of the Wine Route that will captivate you. The first is Harbour Estates Winery. Take Fourth Avenue to Jordan Road, (Route 24), turn left and drive until just before you reach the QEW. (On the way you might want to stop at Niagara Presents, which carries an exclusive line of Niagara-sourced food products — great for picnics and gifts.)

HARBOUR ESTATES

When a farm credit advisor opens a winery you know he's done his home-work and he's confident about his investment. Fraser Mowat had grown tender fruit on his 50-acre farm in Jordan Station for 20 years. Marketing problems in the early nineties turned his sights to other ways to earn a living. He and his wife already had a uniquely warm site 30 feet above Jordan Harbour (where the Twenty Mile Creek enters Lake Ontario) with good air drainage and air movement from both the harbour and the lake, so it made sense to convert their orchard into a vineyard. The vineyard now produces 29 acres of Cabernet Franc, Cabernet Sauvignon and Merlot. By 2001 they plan to have completed a wine centre, restaurant, docking facilities, trail systems and a patio to watch sunsets on the harbour. Harbour Estates can be seen as you cross Jordan Harbour on the QEW between Plain and Fancy Restaurant and The Beacon. Look south. Where the land pokes into the harbour at the closest point is Harbour Estates. For an alternative tour of the Jordan wineries, take the Jordan exit off the QEW and reverse the order presented in this chapter.

Take Jordan Road to Fourth Avenue and continue to Thirteenth Street. Go north to reach the Thirteenth Street Winery.

THIRTEENTH STREET

The name, Thirteenth Street Winery, conjures up a defiant neighbourhood in the Bronx, but nothing could be further from the truth. This is Niagara's wine country at its countriest.

A "winery of their own" was the natural consequence for a group of prize-winning amateur winemakers who had been meeting on a regular basis. However

On Jordan's Main Street

Thirteenth Street Winery

Niagara Presents
4000 Jordan Road
Jordan Station, Ontario, L0R 1S0
Tel: 905-562-1907
Fax: 905-562-0182
Exclusive line of specialty jams, jellies, condiments and vinegars created by Niagara cooks using only the highest-quality Niagara-grown produce.

RECOMMENDED PRODUCERS

Thirteenth Street Winery
3938 Thirteenth Street
Jordan Station, Ontario, L0R 1S0
Tel: 905-562-9463
Fax: 905-562-
Small is beautiful. Open Saturdays, but phone first. You're in for a treat in hand-crafted wines.

Creekside Estate Winery

Creekside Estate Winery
2170 Fourth Avenue
Jordan Station, Ontario, LOR 1S0
Tel: 905-562-0035
Fax: 905-562-5493
E-mail: creeksidewines@aol.com
www.creeksideestatewinery.com
Annual production: 15,500 cases
Aussie winemaker Marcus Ansems is creating some very interesting Rieslings, Sauvignon Blancs, Chardonnays and Merlots. Picnic area overlooking Sixteen Mile Creek. Bucolic, unrushed. Lots of personal attention.

they all wanted to retain their respective day jobs, so they set parameters on how large they would become.

The partners soon grouped themselves into grower/winemaker clusters, each with its own label: Gunther Funk and Herb Jacobson make wine from Funk's Jordan Station farm under the G.H. Funk label. Erv Willms and Ken Douglas source their fruit from Erv's Niagara-on-the-Lake vineyard under the Sandstone label. A fifth partner is Deborah Paskus, who is both grower and winemaker, leasing 8-10 acres from other vineyards in Niagara.

The winery is located on Funk's Thirteenth Street vineyard. Each partner puts in base materials and shares the winemaking facility. Their intention is to craft wines and have total control over what they produce. To crank up production would mean losing control. The up side is that their wines are among the very finest in Canada — sparkling Rieslings, Rieslings, Chardonnays and Gamays that are sure to impress and unforgettable Pinot Noirs. This is the Williams and Selym of Niagara. The down side is they intend to stay at 1,600 cases. Get there early.

CREEKSIDE ESTATE WINERY
Along Fourth Avenue to the west of Thirteenth Street is Creekside Estate Winery. Proprietors Peter Jensen, with his background in the brewing

Vintage House

ACCOMMODATIONS

Vintage House
3853 Main Street
Jordan, Ontario, L0R 1S0
Tel: 905-562-3441
Fax: 905-562-3441
E-mail: vintage@vaxxine.com
www.v-ip.com/vintage
Victorian house (1840s) located in the
historic town of Jordan. Private guest rooms
surrounded by gardens, furnished with
antiques. Full breakfast. Directly across the
street from On the Twenty and Cave Spring
Cellars Winery. Rates: $110-$125.

The Willows Bed and Breakfast
4014 Nineteenth Street
Jordan, Ontario, L0R 1S0
Tel: 905-562-5031
Fax; 905-562-7082
www.v-ip.com/willows
Within walking distance to Jordan Village.
Ensuite, private, non-smoking — a ravine view
of Twenty Mile Creek. Private bath, full break-
fast, 3 acres of landscaped gardens. Rates:
$95.

business, and wife Laura McCain Jensen, who was experienced in food marketing from the distinguished McCain Foods family of New Brunswick, purchased a hobbled V.P. Cellars, renamed it Creekside Estate, and began to turn the little winery around. They expanded the production area, established a barrel program and lured Aussie winemaker, Marcus Ansems, to run things. With Ansems' know-how, a concern for the preservation of fruit, and a focus on the creation of silky textured wines, a new tone had been set, particularly with Merlot and Cabernet Sauvignon and the aromatic whites (off-dry Riesling, Sauvignon Blanc).

The Jensen-McCain duo own two properties in Nova Scotia in the verdant Annapolis Valley, producing some of Nova Scotia's first vinifera (Chardonnay and Pinot Noir at Habitant Winery and Pereau Vineyards). Their next project is an ultra-premium winery in Niagara-on-the-Lake. Visit Creekside Estate, bring a picnic or order one by calling ahead and enjoy lunch along the banks of Sixteen Mile Creek.

PELHAM/ST. CATHARINES

Although there are only two wineries in this part of Niagara, the area is the focal point of the peninsula and worth a visit. Pelham is the geographical centre of Niagara, with a centrepiece at the Fonthill Kame, the highest elevation in the region. The surrounding falls are quite bucolic. St. Catharines is the largest urban centre (130,000 pop.) and has numerous restaurants, accommodations and points of interest, (e.g. Rodmen Hall Art Centre, Port Dalhousie, Welland Canal, Brock University Centre for the Performing Arts.)

PELHAM

HENRY OF PELHAM FAMILY ESTATE WINERY

The American Revolution created not one new country, but two — the United States and Canada. The end of the war directly resulted in the settling of the Niagara Peninsula. Land was granted to refugees and soldiers alike. American refugees loyal to the Crown made the arduous trek north. Over 600 soldiers and their families decided to stay in the area rather than return to the United States where they could expect a very hostile reception. Senior officers received 1,000 acres, captains 700, junior officers 500, sergeants 200, and privates 100, with 50 additional acres granted for each dependant. Even buglers could petition for lands, which is precisely what Nicholas Smith did and was granted. He soon sold his original parcel and purchased a better plot at the crossroads where the three Townships of Louth, Pelham and Thorold came together. His son, Henry Smith, inherited the land in 1842 on which he built an inn.

Top: *Statue of William Hamilton Merritt*

RECOMMENDED PRODUCERS

Henry of Pelham Family Estate Winery
1469 Pelham Road
St. Catharines, Ontario, L2R 6P7
Tel: 905-684-8423
Fax: 905-684-8444
E-mail: winery@henryofpelham.com
www.henryofpelham.com
Annual production: 60,000 cases
Besides offering very fine wines, they plan some of the more innovative activities for wine enthusiasts during touring season (e.g. Shakespeare in the Vineyard, hiking on the Bruce Trail). Check out their web site. Not to be missed.

Henry of Pelham Family Estate Winery

One hundred and sixty years later, in 1988, Henry Smith's relatives converted the inn, once the setting for large public dances, fairs and social gatherings, into a winery. Although cars have replaced teams of waiting horses, and wine has replaced lager, it is as if its destiny as a crossroads intended to bring people together has continued unbroken. Today that same inn houses the offices, tasting rooms and retail store of the Henry of Pelham Family Estate Winery.

The winery and its 100 acres of surrounding vineyards, is owned by Henry Smith's relatives, the fifth generation of Smiths, the Speck brothers — Paul, Matthew and Daniel Speck. As teenagers they planted the vineyard adjacent to the winery. As adults they have guided the business to a 60,000 case operation producing some of Canada's finest premium wines. Winemaker Ron Giesbrecht is meticulous, creating early drinking wines of unoaked Chardonnay and Sauvignon Blanc, along with rich barrel-aged Chardonnays that keep their lively character ten years and more. His real genius is for reds. Giesbrecht has found a way to give new meaning to the category of French hybrid. His Baco Noir Reserves spend extended time in oak, giving them a toasty character and robust personality. His Cabernet blends are also extraordinary.

Henry of Pelham has a full schedule of activities. Particularly popular is Shakespeare in the Vineyard, where a troop of actors perform outdoors. So popular has the event become that the Specks are considering taking it to other parts of the region.

FONTHILL AND THE SHORT HILLS

Fonthill is a small village located in the Town of Pelham, named after the kame that defines the complex topography that differentiates it sharply from the rest of Niagara. (A kame is a giant hill, in this case 75 metres high, composed of sand and gravel deposited from the water of a melted glacier.) The Fonthill Kame exerts considerable influence on the climate of Pelham, sheltering it from prevailing winds from the southwest, thus providing beneficial growing conditions for tender fruit crops. The gently rolling Short Hills to the north of Fonthill contain meandering freshwater streams and steep-sided valleys that provide some of the most picturesque country-side in southern Ontario.

Some of the Short Hills have been preserved as the Short Hills Provincial Park. What sets this park apart is the existence of preserves of the almost extinct Carolinian forest. Besides the Niagara Escarpment, this 688-hectare park is one of the most extensively forested areas in Niagara. Much

Springbank House

of the forest has remained undisturbed for decades with stands of Carolinian black walnut, black maple, hemlock and beech. Bring along your walking shoes and a picnic lunch. There are spots that are irresistible for their sheer serenity and beauty. Access to many of the park's trails is from Gilligan Road.

The Town of Pelham is known for the dozens of sixth generation Century Farms. These are farms that have been operated by six unbroken generations. The Horton Farm on Balfour Street is typical. The farm was built in 1870 after the original log cabin was burned. The Horton family history tells of children being tied to trees to keep them out of danger while logs were being felled and hewn to make the original home.

THE COMFORT MAPLE
Drive along Balfour Street and turn east onto Metler Road. A few metres from the intersection on your right-hand side, is a small sign by the side of

ACCOMMODATIONS

Springbank House
68 Yates Street
St. Catharines, Ontario, L2R 5R8
Tel: 905-641-1713
Fax: 905-641-7557
E-mail: kathyt@springbankhouse.com
www.springbankhouse.com
Built in 1905 on the site of the famous Springbank Hotel. Luxury spa of the mid-1800s. Queen Anne Revival, stately home, antique furnishings. Comfortable walking distance from heart of downtown St. Catharines and Montebello Park.
Rates: $99-$150.

a long drive announcing The Comfort Maple. At the end of the drive is the 500-year-old majestic maple tree the Comfort family used to call "old Glory." It is estimated that this tree was a sapling when Columbus discovered America, and 100 years old when Champlain set foot in Canada. It reaches a height of 34 metres (112 feet) with a trunk circumference of almost 6 metres (20 feet) just before it divides into two main branches. The crown forms almost a complete circle extending about 36 metres (118 feet) and spreads 15 to 30 centimetres (96 to 12 inches) a year. Because the tree developed in the open, it has spread freely. Its leaves are smaller than other maples of its kind, but there are few trees in the world that will fill you with as much awe.

This majestic maple was accepted for preservation by the Niagara Peninsula Conservation authority at the request of the Comfort family, who still own the surrounding land, much as their ancestors have since 1816.

ST. JOHN'S CONSERVATION AREA
The St. John's Conservation Area is one of the last remaining public areas left in Ontario to view, firsthand, the over 400 species of plants that grow in the Carolinian Zone. Although it is a small area, only 78 acres, it has never been used extensively and rare species have remained intact. Also, there are trees over 200 years old that missed the settlers' axe.

Besides sassafras, black walnut, butternut and shagbark hickory trees, you'll see wild grape vines spiralling up the tallest trees, stretching for light.

HERNDER ESTATE WINES
The second winery with a rural St. Catharines address is Hernder Estate Wines located down the road from Henry of Pelham, on Eighth Avenue. (For some reason, when the town's eighteenth-century surveyors stamped their rigid grid pattern over Niagara, either they had their sights on developing Niagara into Manhattan, or they lacked the imagination to give the rural concession lines actual names. In St. Catharines, for instance, the numbered avenues go east and west, while streets go north and south. Contrary to the density of urban centres, few if any of these streets and avenues have more than three or four farms located on them.)

Hernder Estates Wines was founded in 1991 by Fred Hernder, a grape farmer with vines in the family since 1939. Until 1991 their business had consisted of producing grapes and wine supplies for wineries or the home winemaking market. Then they decided to make their own, locating the winery in their historic barn (circa 1867) that they restored, saving the orig-

Harvest Barn fresh produce and baked goods market

inal post-and-beam, split-beam construction and interior stone walls.

Hernder's has become a favourite spot for brides — a wishing pond and well and Niagara's only covered bridge have been added to enhance the property. Hernder's vineyards are among the largest in Niagara, totalling 500 acres. All of their wines are VQA-approved, made from 100 percent Ontario grapes and from between ten to fifteen different grape varieties.

HARVEST ESTATES WINES

"All good things — under one roof." Located adjacent to Niagara's finest fresh produce and baked goods market, Harvest Barn, Harvest Estates produces twelve fruit wines and twenty grape wines. The combination of delicious wines and select fresh products in close proximity makes this an

RECOMMENDED PRODUCERS

Hernder Estate Wines
1607 Eighth Avenue
St. Catharines, Ontario, L2R 6P7
Tel: 905-684-3300
Fax: 905-684-3303
E-mail: wine@vaxxine.com
www.hernder.com
Annual production: 40,000 cases
Charming covered bridge, a function room to accommodate hundreds and century barn make this an attractive site for parties, weddings, etc. Check out their summer barbecues featuring homemade sausage.

Harvest Estates Wines
1179 Fourth Avenue
St. Catharines, Ontario
Tel: 905-682-0080
Fax: 905-684-3303
Email: wine@vaxxine.com

ACCOMMODATIONS

Hayocks on the Lake
43 Ann Street
St. Catharines, Ontario, L2N 5E9
Tel: 905-934-7106
Fax: 905-934-7106
E-mail: hayocks@sympatico.ca
www.bbcanada.com/hayocks
Beautifully landscaped Port Dalhousie
cottage-style home built in 1860 on Lake
Ontario. Walking distance from historic Port
Dalhousie and Lakeside Park and beach.
Near Henley Regatta.
Rates: $75-$150.

Keaton Manor
1590 Regional Road 81
St. Catharines, Ontario, L2R 6P7
Tel: 905-688-6746
Fax: 905-688-0696
Lovely property next to the Niagara
Escarpment. Historic inn built in 1812. Pool.
On the wine route. Rates: $85-$125.

Millpond Bed and Breakfast
1552 Regional Road 81 West
St. Catharines, Ontario, L2R 6P7
Tel: 905-684-6314
Fax: 905-684-6359
www.millpondstudio.com/bb
Located on the wine route, nestled by a
lovely four-acre pond beside the Niagara
Escarpment. Rates $125-$180.

RESTAURANTS

Albert's Restaurant on the Water
61 Lake Street
St. Catharines, Ontario
Tel: 905-646-5000
Situated in old Port Dalhousie, featuring
Spanish and Mediterranean cuisine.

ideal marriage, perhaps one of convenience, but it sure is handy.

It is an interesting concept — the tasting room and retail store is at this location, but their winery facility is 1000 metres to the west. All grape wines have been awarded VQA recognition. Try their Iced Pear and Off-dry Riesling. At the market next door, buy the fixings for a picnic then find a quiet spot for a peaceful lunch. The lake is on the other side of the QEW, two minutes away.

ST. CATHARINES
Return to Regional Highway 81 going east. This takes you straight into St. Catharines, the largest city in the peninsula. Known as "the garden city" it is also the home of the Welland Canal. Regional 81 becomes St. Paul Street West as it crosses Fifth Avenue.

Of cultural and architectural interest is Rodman Hall Arts Centre with a permanent collection of 800 sculptures, paintings and drawings, the majority of which are produced by Canadian artists of the nineteenth and twentieth centuries. Look for the signs to Rodman Hall just before you reach the Twelve Mile Creek bridge. On the other side of the bridge, there's a statue on your right of William Hamilton Merritt, the man who was most instrumental in turning this once sleepy nineteenth-century hamlet into the largest city in the peninsula, with a population of 130,000.

THE WELLAND CANAL

American-born William Hamilton Merritt had a flour mill operation that was failing because of the lack of a reliable supply of water for power. Above the Escarpment to the south, was a stream that he could potentially tap into. In the fall of 1818 he and two other businessmen set off to survey the lands that led to the Welland River to see if it were possible to devise a series of channels or canals that could reach St. Catharines and the Merritt mill.

It soon became obvious that the real source of power wasn't in flour milling, but, rather in the opportunities that lay in navigation. Merritt thought big. If he could find a way to circumnavigate the Escarpment, he could connect the entire trading heartland of the American Midwest to the St. Lawrence and then the Atlantic. Markets in Europe were just a crossing

The Blue Mermaid
10 Market Square
St. Catharines, Ontario
Tel: 905-684-7465
Up-scale in the downtown market square.
Continental cuisine.

Kristin's Fine Cuisine
30 Wellington Street
St. Catharines, Ontario
Tel: 905-682-5022
Bistro style, Provençal menu. Superior dining.
Well done.

Mansion House
5 William Street
St. Catharines, Ontario
Tel: 905-685-5681
William Hamilton Merritt, founder of the Welland Canal, had his office in the back room. Go here for pub grub and a beer. Much hasn't changed. Good fun.

Port Mansion Theatre Restaurant
12 Lakeport Street
St. Catharines, Ontario
Tel: 905-934-0575
In the heart of old Port Dalhousie, where the first lock of the Welland Canal began. Great theatre. Fun summer town. Lots to see, do.

Pow Wow's
165 St. Paul Street
St. Catharines, Ontario
Tel: 905-934-0575
One of my very favourites. Good food. Fine service. Reasonable prices. Comfortable, fun.

Strega Cafe
19 King Street
St. Catharines, Ontario
Tel: 905-984-5872
Another favourite. Good cooking, pleasant surroundings, moderate prices. Mediterranean-style fare. Open Sundays and weekdays. Take home frozen meals for the work-weary cook.

away. With the threat of lost business by the opening of the Erie Barge Canal to New York City, it was conceivable Montreal could lose markets entirely.

By 1824 Merritt had formed the Welland Canal Company that would eventually secure enough private investors to start digging a system of thirty-nine locks to raise and lower ships over the Escarpment, connecting them to Lake Erie and Lake Ontario. The first canal was completed in 1829 and was considered a wonder of human ingenuity. Since then, three other canals have been constructed to accommodate larger vessels. Industries sprang up along each new location, leaving those towns bypassed to languish.

PORT DALHOUSIE

The village of Port Dalhousie was the location of the first lock as ships entered the canal from Lake Ontario. It survived three out of four incarnations of the canal. At one time its beach was the site of the famous Lakeside Park, which closed in the 1970s. By the time the fourth canal arrived, the village was bypassed and faded like the other towns sharing the same fate. But not for long. Today its resort-style ambience makes it a favourite summer spot for beach-goers, picnickers, sailors, pub-crawlers and summer theatre-goers.

Visible reminders of the previous canals overlap in the Port Dalhousie harbour today. You can see the remains of the locks from the second and third canals and the old customs house. At the turn of the century, Port Dalhousie moored so many ships in its yards, it is said a person could walk the entire width of the canal by jumping from deck to deck amidst a "sea of masts." Passers-by were so close to schooners and steamers they could almost shake hands with the sailors on deck.

Visiting the marina, taking a walk on the pier to the outer lighthouse, dining in the restaurants and shopping in the boutiques are all delightful ways to spend an afternoon. For an advantaged view of locks of the modern canal, visit the St. Catharines Historical Museum at Lock 3 and learn more about the drama of this wonder firsthand from the viewing platform. Here are the twin locks where oceangoing vessels meet, are raised or lowered, and pass in the night ... day, too. Inside the museum is an interpretive centre that provides insight into the canals' early days.

From Lock 3, take a walk or jog alongside the Welland Canal Recreation Trail, a 9-kilometre (5.6-mile) stretch along the west side of the canal. By car you can drive the entire length of the canal from Port Weller on Lake Ontario to Port Colborne on Lake Erie.

HENLEY ISLAND

Henley Island is the home of the Royal Canadian Henley Regatta, established in 1880. With the exception of two years during World War I, it has run continuously ever since. It has full international facilities, a 2,000-metre (2,187-yard) course and a covered grandstand that seats 3,000 spectators. In 1998 it hosted the World Rowing Competitions. If you're a rowing enthusiast, set aside the first week in August for the Henley Regatta.

View of Port Dalhousie's Harbour

Stunning Joe Banks
127 Queenston Street
St. Catharines, Ontario
Tel: 905-687-9798
This is where you go for a very wide selection of the world's greatest beers and a fine selection of Ontario wines.

Wellington Court
11 Wellington Street
St. Catharines, Ontario
Tel: 905-682-5518
Another favourite. I go here whenever I want to celebrate. Fine dining. Small and cosy atmosphere. Niagara at its very best.

PLACES OF INTEREST

Montebello Park
Corners of Ontario, Lake and Queen streets
Mid-nineteenth-century park designed by Olmstead, the designer of Central Park.

Farmers' Market
Downtown St. Catharines on King Street. Every Tuesday, Thursday and Saturday mornings.

Welland Canals Centre at Lock 3 and St. Catharines Museum
Canal Road at Lock 3
Tel: 905-688-5601 or 1-800-305-5134
The Welland Canal is one of the world's greatest engineering triumphs. See the ships "climb the mountain." Explore the fascinating story of the Welland Canals and the unique history of St. Catharines in the museum. Great spot for viewing and learning.

NIAGARA-ON-THE-LAKE

"The prettiest town in Canada"

Niagara-on-the-Lake is reached by taking the QEW east to the Niagara-on-the-Lake exit. Follow the signs to town.

Contrary to what its contemporary moniker attests, Niagara-on-the-Lake is more than just a "pretty" town. It is elegant, historic and carries with it a subtle geophysical energy that makes you feel good while you're there.

To understand Niagara-on-the-Lake, you need to think of it as being two places: the historic old village centre in which the birth of Ontario took shape, and the surrounding "town" or municipality that includes the pre-amalgamation (1970) villages of Virgil, St. David's and Queenston.

Niagara-on-the-Lake — the village centre — is the stately result of its several incarnations as a military stronghold, a sanctuary for homeless American refugees, a legislative centre, a port and shipbuilding hub and a resort and cultural mecca. Each of these lifetimes manifests itself in the village's architecture and traditions.

Forts Mississauga and George testify to its life as a strategic military bastion at one end of the portage route around Niagara Falls, first held by the French in 1726 then captured by the British in 1759. Twenty years later, at the outbreak of the American Revolutionary War, it became a haven to hundreds of homeless American refugees who were loyal to Britain during the conflict.

Left: *Courthouse, Queen Street*   Top: *Clock Tower*

PLACES OF INTEREST

Queenston Park and Brock's Monument
Tel: 905-468-6614
Guided tours of the historic battlefield are available by reservation.

MacKenzie Heritage Printery Museum
1 Queenston Street
Queenston, Ontario, L0S 1J0
Tel: 905-262-5676
www.niagaraparks.com
A joint venture with the Niagara Parks Commission, the printery is the only museum in Canada devoted to displaying historic presses and other equipment covering more than 500 years of the letterpress era. Eight presses, all in working order, demonstrate the sharp contrast between the labour-intensive letterpress method and today's high-speed desktop publishing.

Americans on the other side of the border, still flush with victory over Britain, decided they would complete their manifest destiny to push their boundaries to include all of British North America (Canada). In 1812 they invaded Upper Canada through Queenston Heights in an attempt to capture Niagara-on-the-Lake (then called Newark), which by then had established itself as the legislative centre of the province. Although that battle was won by the defending British army under the leadership of General Brock, Brock lost his life. A monument to that loss was raised at Queenston Heights to commemorate his leadership and valour. The Americans, not to be denied, invaded again, this time occupying Niagara-on-the-Lake for several months, intending to use Fort George as a bridgehead from which the rest of Upper Canada would be invaded. When the fortunes of the war started to turn against the Americans, they had no choice but to retreat. In an act of petulance, however, they burned the town to the ground on their way out.

Supported by the government from claims for "War Losses," the people of Niagara-on-the-Lake rebuilt the village from the ashes and smouldering foundations of their former homes and businesses. Opponents argued that it was silly to preserve the old, and that a new site should be developed.

70 Platoff Street

However, within a decade the town flourished once again. Its homes today are classic examples of Victorian, Regency and Edwardian architecture, many lavished with detailing proudly added by early craftsmen.

Niagara-on-the-Lake is a place of firsts. It was here that Colonel John Butler, the dauntless leader of the famous colonial regiment, Butler's Rangers took the first census in Canada in 1782. The first gristmill in Ontario was built here in 1783 and the first legislature in Upper Canada held its sessions in 1792. At the urging of Colonel John Simcoe, Upper Canada's first lieutenant governor, the legislature abolished the importation of slaves in 1793, which gradually made Upper Canada a refuge for thousands of African-Americans. Niagara-on-the-Lake also had the first newspaper, the first agricultural society and the first public library, where the Law Society of Upper Canada was founded.

The Shaw Festival Theatre, a professional repertory company operating seven months a year with three theatres (the Festival Theatre, Royal George and The Courthouse), is world-renowned, however it is a relatively recent manifestation of Niagara-on-the-Lake's importance as a cultural centre. By the mid-1800s the village was a thriving summer retreat for American tourists and lovers of learning with the establishment of a Chatauqua cultural centre that attracted hundreds of people who came to worship, reflect, paint, listen to poetry and debate.

Throughout its history, Niagara-on-the-Lake has rallied through economic downturns, but it keeps those darker days to itself. There are no reminders of the times when the town was limp with apathy and economic depression. Its current polish is relatively recent. Trickles of tourism had kept it alive, but, with the exception of a few shops to keep its summer residents supplied, there was little commerce to sustain its economy.

Its renaissance began in the sixties. The Shaw Festival was the first to inject vitality into Niagara-on-the-Lake. As the festival grew, the streetscape, fortunately kept intact by earlier benign neglect, started to come alive with interesting shops to keep the theatre-goers' interest piqued between plays. By the seventies a second wave of enthusiasm for the charm of this old Ontario village began and continues today, prompted by the birth of the modern wine industry. But make no mistake, although visitors stake claim to the old town every summer, it remains a living community of 7,000 residents. As much as the town has been gussied up, the townsfolk still catch up on the local gossip at the post office and the bakery and they still scrap out their differences in town council, waging the perennial battle between the forces of preservation and those of development.

The Shaw Festival

Box Office 10 Queen's Parade
Niagara-on-the-Lake, Ontario, L0S 1J0
Tel: 905-468-2172/800-511-7429
Fax: 905-468-3804
www.shawfest.sympatico.ca
The Shaw Festival is the second-largest repertory company in North America and the only theatre in the world that specializes in plays written by Bernard Shaw and his contemporaries (1856-1950). There are three stages on which the company puts on its annual productions. Not to be missed.

Whirlpool Jet Boat Tours

P.O. Box 1215
61 Melville Street
Niagara-on-the-Lake, Ontario, L0S 1J0
Tel: 1-888-438-4444
www.whirlpooljet.com
For something a little different, take a jet boat tour of the Niagara River and see the awe-inspiring Niagara gorge from the water up.

Church Rectory

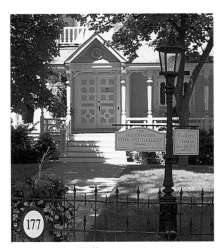

Presentation Gallery

Fort George
Tel: 905-468-4257
Fax: 905-468-4638
E-mail: ont.niagara@pch.gc.ca
www.niagara.com/~parkscan
Built over 200 years ago by the British Army to
defend the vital Niagara frontier and the vulner-
able water communications route from
American invasion. Tours, demonstrations, drills.

FESTIVALS AND EVENTS

Wine Council of Ontario
110 Hanover Drive, Suite B205
St. Catharines, Ontario, L2W 1A4
Tel: 905-684-8070 or 1-888-5-WINERY
Fax: 905-684-2993
www.wineroute.com
All the wineries of Niagara have special
plans to make a summer excursion you'll
never forget. Each winery has something
different. Get a brochure outlining all events
at the Wine Council.

Tastes of Niagara
P.O. Box 22005
Town and Country Plaza
Niagara Fall, Ontario, L2J 4J3
Tel: 905-357-6104
Fax: 905-357-5838

Niagara-on-the-Lake's historic Queen Street includes the Niagara Apothecary, which operated as a pharmacy from 1819 to 1971. Now converted into a museum, it displays the old cures and formulations once in fashion.

The clock tower in the heart of Queen Street was first designed in 1922 to commemorate the men from the village who were lost in World War I; those lost in World War II were added.

The courthouse on Queen Street was built around 1847 as the county seat of the Niagara District. When the seat was moved to St. Catharines in 1862 it became the town hall until it outgrew its space and became a perfect venue for the first performances of the Shaw Festival.

Most of the buildings on Queen are historic structures, each with an intriguing history. McLelland's West End Store at 106 Queen was built around 1835, when shipbuilding was at its peak. This Classic Revival store sold provisions, as the large "T" sign above the door conveys.

A walk into the residential part of the village reveals historic homes and gardens, lovingly restored examples of some of the finest examples of nineteenth-century architecture. Presentation Gallery at 177 King Street is a fine example of a stately Victorian home with filigree and turrets typical of the time. Today, it is the gallery for noted artists Trisha Romance, Alex Colville and Phillip Craig.

Fort George, built by the British in 1796 to guard the entrance of the Niagara River, played a strategic role in the War of 1812, but was burned by Americans in 1813 during their retreat. The fort was restored to its original specifications in the 1930s. All eleven buildings of the original fourteen are furnished as they were from 1797 to 1813.

Inside the fort, costumed staff bring to life the early days of the nineteenth century. Outside, uniformed soldiers drill and prepare for battle. Every July there is also a re-enactment of artillery bombardment by invading forces.

The Niagara Historical Museum on Castlereagh Street was founded in 1895 and was the first in Ontario to be built solely as a museum. It contains over 20,000 artifacts and is a mother lode of local history, walking tours, displays and information.

The second way to think about Niagara-on-the-Lake is in terms of the "town" or municipality that surrounds the outskirts of the village. This is the wine country of Niagara-on-the-Lake. There are three routes along which the wineries can be explored: the Niagara Parkway that parallels the Niagara River; Highway 55, the main route into the old town; or the meandering Lakeshore Road that follows the scenic shoreline of Lake Ontario.

The Niagara Apothecary

E-mail: tastes@vaxxine.com
Usually the third Saturday in August, an alliance of wineries, chefs and local food producers holds a wine and food fest at Queenston Heights Park. Chefs pool their talents with local producers and showcase the best of Niagara cuisine. A Niagara must do. Terrific.

RECOMMENDED PRODUCERS

Inniskillin Wines, Inc.
R. R. #1
Niagara Parkway and Line 3
Niagara-on-the-Lake, Ontario, L0S 1J0
Tel: 905-468-2187
Fax: 905-468-3554
E-mail: inniskil@inniskillin.com
www.inniskillin.com
Annual Production: 160,000 cases
Self-guided or tutored tours of the winery are outstanding. Tasting room and retail shop fully staffed. Known worldwide for Icewine, however, Pinot Noir and Chardonnay are also very delicious.

TOUR 1: THE WINERIES ALONG THE NIAGARA PARKWAY

Sir Winston Churchill called it "the prettiest Sunday afternoon drive in the world." This peaceful 46-kilometre (25-mile) stretch follows the Niagara River from Niagara-on-the-Lake to Fort Erie. It is perfect picnic country, complemented by fresh fruit and homemade goods from any one of the numerous fruit stands that line the route. The paved recreation trail (2.5 metres/8 feet wide) is ideal for joggers, walkers, bicyclists, wheelchairists and in-line skaters. Along this romantic road is a cavalcade of regal homes, historical museums and beautiful views of the river with many century trees under whose limbs time warps at a manageable and rejuvenating pace.

INNISKILLIN WINES

It is not by chance we start our tour here. For it was along the Niagara Parkway that the modern wine industry of Ontario was launched. On July 31, 1975, Inniskillin Wines was incorporated, and its founders, Donald Ziraldo and Karl Kaiser, were granted the first winery license in Ontario since 1930. Inniskillin took its name from the famous Irish regiment, the Inniskilling fusiliers who served in the War of 1812. The vineyard was the original Crown land granted to the regiment's Colonel on completion of his military service.

Right: *Inniskillin Winery*

The historic Brae Burn Barn, constructed in the 1920s, is thought to be designed by Frank Lloyd Wright, and now houses the retail store and gallery.

Most interesting about Inniskillin Wines, Inc. is their self-guided tour that outlines in a series of stations the history of Inniskillin Wines, Inc., plus provides background on cool climate viticulture, the Vintners' Quality Alliance, grape varieties grown in Ontario, harvesting, cooperage, wine-making and barrel-aging. It is a one-stop source of education and fine wines. Particularly notable are their Pinot Noirs, Cabernet Francs, Chardonnays, Pinot Grigios and their award-winning and distinctive sparkling Icewine. Quite voluptuous. Inniskillin is now part of Vincor, Ltd., the fourth largest wine company in North America and Canada's largest.

REIF ESTATE WINERY

At the Niagara Parkway, make a left. A short hop away is Reif Estate Winery, directly on the Parkway.

Reif Estate Winery was opened in 1983 with a promise to emphasize the vineyard in all their work. Klaus W. Reif, president, has a degree in viticulture and oenology from Geisenheim University in Germany. Of interest is his attention to the impact of cloning on wine flavour. Reif's Rieslings are a good example of this dedication. He isolates three separate Riesling clones (one French and two German), vinifies them the same, then notes their finer distinctions in flavour. Reif also produces a hefty Bordeaux-styled Cabernet called Tesoro with classic notes of chocolate, leather, cedar and mint. He and co-winemaker Roberto De Dominico, team up to produce

Reif Estate Winery
R.R. #2
15608 Niagara Parkway
Niagara-on-the-Lake, Ontario, L0S 1J0
Tel: 905-468-7738
Fax: 905-468-5616
E-mail: wine@reifwinery.com
www.reifwinery.com
Annual Production: 35,000 cases
Located directly on the scenic Niagara Parkway, special interest in Chardonnays, Rieslings and barrel-aged Bordeaux-style reds.

some very interesting Chardonnays and sweet wines, with a special deftness with Lake Harvest Riesling and Icewine.

MARYNISSEN ESTATES LTD.

John Marynissen, originally from the Netherlands, settled in Niagara-on-the-Lake in the early fifties, growing mostly tender fruit until he decided to plant vinifera grapes in the seventies. He was the first to plant Cabernet Sauvignon in Canada and now has the oldest block. Although he makes some delicious whites, (Sur Lie Chardonnay, etc.), Marynissen is best known for his premium reds.

Daughter Sandra Marynissen has taken on the responsibility of managing the business and has slowly started to make award-winning wine of her own. Especially interesting is their attention to the differing terroir of their two lots. Lot sixty-six, the heavier soilm, produces red wines with more richly concentrated flavour. Lot 31, which is sandier, produces a lighter style. Interesting to compare. Marynissen Estates prices its wines very reasonably for the quality they produce.

LAILEY VINEYARDS

Just north of Reif Estates, along the beautiful Niagara Parkway and across from the historic McFarland House, is Lailey Vineyards. David and Donna Lailey began their vineyard in the seventies, when they purchased the land from David's father. At that time it was mostly cherries, pears, plums and peaches. The young couple, both teachers, very quickly learned how to farm

Marynissen Estates Ltd.
R.R. #6
Concession 1
Niagara-on-the-Lake, Ontario, L0S 1J0
Tel: 905-468-7270
Fax: 905-468-5784
E-mail: marynisn@netcom.ca
Annual Production: 10,000 cases
Well-made reds, smaller artisanal production. Especially worth trying are Cabernet Sauvignon and Cabernet Franc. Some of the oldest Cabernet vines in Canada.

Lailey Vineyards
15940 Niagara Parkway
Niagara-on-the-Lake, Ontario, L0S 1J0
Tel: 905-468-0503
Fax: 905-468-8012
Email: tonya@laileyvineyard.com
www.laileyvineyard.com

Left: *Lailey Vineyards*

grapes. In the early years there were few people who could advise them on growing better quality varieties, so through trial and error, planting and replanting, they learned how to produce premium quality fruit. Soon, they transformed their vineyards using a canopy management system that proved right for their growing conditions. Combined with other practices such as hand harvesting, that began their journey to producing fruit of uncommon depth and character.

For more than a decade they sold some of their Chardonnay and Pinot Noir grapes to local wineries, and processed the rest to sell premium juice to home winemakers. Always active on numerous community Boards of Directors, Donna was the grower representative on the founding board of the VQA, and has always been steadfast in her belief in the potential the Niagara Peninsula has to produce fine wines, fruits and vegetables. For many years, Derek Barnett made award-winning wines from Lailey Vineyards fruit while he was winemaker at Southbrook Estates winery. He has joined Lailey Vineyards as their winemaker. In 2000, Donna and David formed a winery on their property with their daughter Tonya and her husband Dr. Yves Starreveld, plus winemaker Derek Barnett and his wife Judith.

The location on the Parkway is beautiful, the wines already have a track record for quality, and the people are some of the nicest you'll meet in Niagara. Call for an appointment.

PELLER ESTATES WINERY

Peller Estates Winery must be on any tour to Niagara's wine country. It is twenty-five acres of vineyards that surround a gorgeous 5,000 sq.ft. facility made in a Canadian Provincial style. The spacious entry looks more like a Ralais lobby with a large fireplace. It is flanked by stylish, overstuffed couches and chairs and a painting of Andrew Peller, who started the original business in the early 1960s (Andres; Hillebrand). The building has three main features: a stunning tasting room and retail store to the left; a barrel cellar downstairs; and an artfully decorated dinning room above. Peller Estates is a visitor's dream. An outdoor patio surrounding the main building engages more casual dining.

The facility is situated in a way that captures an inspiring view of the Niagara Escarpment. As beautiful as the setting is, the wines are its equal, and they are only available at the winery. The style of their predominantly single-varietal reds such as Cabernet Sauvignon, Cabernet Franc and Merlot are bold, fruit-forward, New World–styled wines. Deeply extracted and

Peller Estates Winery
290 John Street East
Niagara-on-the-Lake, Ontario, L0S 1J0
Tel: 905-468-4678 / 1-888-673-5537
Fax: 905-468-1920
Email: info@peller.com
www.peller.com

Left: *Peller Estates Winery*

Château des Charmes
P.O. Box 280
1025 York Road
Niagara-on-the-Lake, Ontario, L0S 1J0
Tel: 905-262-4219
Fax: 905-262-5548
E-mail: pabosc@chateaudescharmes.com
www.chateaudescharmes.com
Annual Production: 100,000 cases
Visit this state-of-the-art facility. It has a well-organized tour plus video, tasting room and retail shop. Of note: Chardonnay, Cabernets, Icewine, Late Harvest and a full-bodied Gamay Noir not to miss.

rich, they drink well now, but hold fine potential to grow into elegant maturity. Whites include Chardonnay, Sauvignon Blanc, Riesling, and Gewurztraminer. The winery restaurant upstairs is splendid. The cuisine, built around fresh local produce, is exceptional.

Peller Estates can be reached by taking the Niagara Parkway to John Street and turning left. The winery is near the corner on the left. If you're already in the village of Niagara-on-the-Lake, find the Pillar and Post Inn and Conference Centre on John Street and turn left.

Château des Charmes

In 1978, Paul Michel Bosc, a fifth-generation French winemaker and winegrower, founded Château des Charmes. Since the sixties he had served as senior oenologist at one of Ontario's larger wineries at the time, Château Gai (now part of the Vincor group). His gift to the Ontario wine industry is one that continues to reap benefits. Not only was he a pathfinder who believed Ontario could grow vinifera grapes when even local scientists at the research station thought otherwise, he was the first to dedicate himself to the fledging industry — especially during periods when most of the grape-growing community in Niagara was literally pulling up vines, terribly threatened by the impending impact of free trade. Contrary to their pessimism, Bosc believed it would be a boon to the industry, forcing growers into producing better quality. Not a man to relish the limelight, Bosc nevertheless accepted the uneasy crown as Grape King in 1988 in order to temper the industry's predictions of doom. He prevailed.

His other gift has been his dedication to research — to continually explore the ways in which better clones can be established that are best suited to cool climatic conditions. One of his spectacular achievements is the recent development of a Gamay Noir clone, Gamay Droit or Upright, known for its upright growing nature on the vine. It produces wine of uncommon concentration of both colour, and flavour. Look for it.

Other wines are the St. David's Bench and Paul Bosc Estate vineyard-designated series of Bordeaux reds and Chardonnays. A fine touring facility hosting tours on a regular basis, Château des Charmes is another must on your itinerary.

Maleta Vineyards and Estate Winery
450 Queenston Road, R.R.#4
Niagara-on-the-Lake, L0S 1J0
Tel: 905-685-8486
Fax: 905-685-7998
Email: vyntnr@vaxxine.com

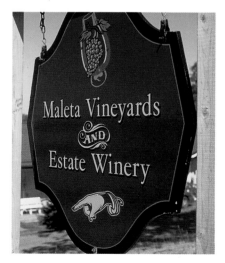

MALETA VINEYARDS AND ESTATE WINERY
Car dealer Stan Maleta couldn't resist the pull of his passion to make wine, so he bought a small block of land not far from Château des Charmes, on the original sight of a heritage winery from the twenties, called Sunniholm.

It's impossible to miss. Look for pink buildings at the bottom of a hill. His wines include a Meritage (Bordeaux blend), Reserve Chardonnay, Reserve Gamay Noir, Reserve Riesling (which captured a world spotlight in a German international award) and a rosé.

Meleta has the best selection of wine books in the Peninsula. Marilyn Maleta is a sales rep for a wine book distributor, and as such, she has access to the best. She has also designed a souvenir Wines of Ontario poster. Call for an appointment.

TOUR 2: WINERIES ALONG HIGHWAY 55
HILLEBRAND ESTATES WINERY, LTD.

Hillebrand Estates, established in 1979, has a well-structured wine tour that includes an explanation of sparkling wine production using the classic traditional method, plus a stunning retail shop and tasting room, and, most distinctive of all the wineries in Niagara-on-the-Lake, a winery restaurant dedicated to menus on based seasonal foods sourced from Niagara farms.

Hillebrand Estates boasts the largest product list of VQA wines in Canada, sourcing fruit for their premium lines from vineyards throughout Niagara. Notable are the wines in the Trius series, includes selected Rieslings, a Cabernet blend, Chardonnay and a brut, Chardonnay-based sparkling wine. This elegant series is made for long life as is their ultra-premium limited Showcase Series. Both drink well young, but the real rewards come when they are given a chance to develop complexity and depth.

Hillebrand Estates Winery
R.R. #2
Highway 55
Niagara-on-the-Lake, Ontario, L0S 1J0
Tel: 905-468-7123/ 1-800-582-8412
Fax: 905-468-4789
E-mail: info@hillebrand.com
www.hillebrand.com
Noteworthy site to visit, taste and dine. Retail store, regular tours, bicycle vineyard tours, music concerts throughout the summer.

Pillitteri Estates Winery
R. R. #2
1696 Highway 55
Niagara-on-the-Lake, Ontario, L0S 1J0
Tel: 905-468-3147
Fax: 905-468-0389
E-mail: winery@pillitteri.com
www.pillitteri.com
Annual Production: 25,000 cases
Original fruit stand, bakery, still part of
winery offerings. Fifty-three acres of family-
estate controlled vines. Full line of
award-winning wines. Of note, Family
Reserve Merlot.

As their viticulturist works with local growers helping them to develop their vineyards, the chef in the Hillebrand's Vineyard Café is equally dedicated to working with local farmers through his "forager" who sources product and contracts the crops the chef requests for his menus. Fabulous! Their vineyard summer music series of jazz, blues and strings concerts is also very popular. Hillebrand Estates products are available in 102 Vineyards retail outlets throughout Ontario since Hillebrand along with Peller Estates, is one of the companies that comprise the family of Andrés Wines, Ltd., Canada's second-largest wine company.

PILLITTERI ESTATES WINERY

Across the highway, a few metres away, is family-run Pillitteri Estates Winery, founded by amateur winemaker Gary Pillitteri, currently a Liberal Member of Parliament. The family's fifty-three acres of vines form the basis for the fruit they source in their wines. Distinctive at Pillitteri is a bakery and a seasonal fruit market and fruit-packing plant, plus an outdoor garden patio. During peak seasons, they offer trolley rides through the vineyard and orchards. One of the few who produces a delightful Pinot Grigio and an unoaked Chardonnay, their Cabernet Franc Family Reserve and Family Reserve Merlot are dazzling. Also interesting is their sparkling, Duemilla, made from Chardonnay and Pinot Noir.

Above left and below: *Pillitteri Estates Winery*

Jackson-Triggs Niagara Estate Winery
2145 Niagara Stone Road
Niagara-on-the-Lake, Ontario, L0S 1J0
Tel: 905-468-4637 / 1-866-589-4637
Fax: 905-468-4673
Email: info@jacksontriggswinery.com
jacksontriggswinery.com

Jackson-Triggs Niagara Estate Winery

In the summer of 2001, Canada's largest wine company Vincor [fourth in North America — and the parent company of Inniskillin, Inniskillin Okanagan, R.H. Phillips (California), Hogue Cellars (Washington, plus several other holdings and subsidiaries] — turned their premium brand, Jackson-Triggs, into one of the most technologically advanced wineries in the country. The brand, named after Vice President Allan Jackson and President and CEO Don Triggs, produced the Jackson-Triggs wine portfolio out of their Niagara Falls facility, once the home of the venerable Brights Wines Ltd. (1893). Giving the brand a home of its own meant sparing nothing. The facility was designed from the ground up to optimize quality, while incorporating the principles of environmental sustainability.

Located on Highway 55, the main artery to the village of Niagara-on-the-Lake, the estate's bold, contemporary structure seems out of place in a town devoted to historic preservation and recreation, until you discover that the facility was inspired by traditional farm buildings, with post and beam frames and a wide "barn door" in the front. Rather than clapboard wood, its materials are a combination of natural stone, native fir trusses and

Jackson-Triggs Niagara Estate Winery

high-tech aluminum framing. Although visitors are welcome, the structure was made for wine making with equipment that provides high levels of flexibility and control.

For instance, it has a three-tiered, gravity flow assisted system to minimize harmful pumping of young wine; open-top fermenters and roto-fermenters for gentle colour extraction for reds; moveable "drainers," and two large barrel cellars. Australian-born Rob Scapin heads a team of winemakers who are steadily building the Jackson-Triggs reputation. Vineyards on the property are still young, but Scapin works closely with a number of independent growers in the Region to augment their signature wines of Merlot, Cabernet Franc, Cabernet Sauvignon and Sauvignon Blanc. Production is expected to exceed 100,000 cases by 2005.

Go for the tour and tasting. It is designed to provide a comprehensive experience that explores all the steps in modern wine making. The end of the tour culminates with a food and wine sensory experience in the Tasting Gallery.

JOSEPH'S ESTATE WINES

In 1979 Joseph Pohorly opened Newark Wines, the third person to open a winery in Niagara-on-the-Lake since Prohibition. He sold in 1982 to German interests and the following year they renamed it Hillebrand Estates. After a ten-year hiatus, the lure of the wine industry tugged at Pohorly, and, with the purchase of a 20-acre vineyard, he was back in business.

Among his varietal vinifera wines (Chardonnay, Pinot Gris, Cabernet),

Joseph's Estate Wines
1811 Niagara Stone Road
Highway 55/R.R.#2
Niagara-on-the-Lake, Ontario, L0S 1J0
Tel: 905-468-1259
Fax: 905-468-3103
E-mail:info@josephsestatewines.com
www.josephsestatewines.com
Annual Production: 20,000 cases
Stop here for a quieter winery stop and lots of personal attention. Interesting examples of Petit Sirah, Pinot Grigio and fruit wines.

Left and below: *Strewn Winery and Wine Country Cooking School*

he makes one of the very few Petit Sirahs in Ontario. He also does well with fruit wines (pear, peach, strawberry, apricot and black cherry). All are very reasonably priced.

TOUR 3: WINERIES ALONG THE LAKESHORE

Lakeshore drive is one of Niagara's secrets — delightfully much less travelled and most serene as it swings with the contours of the lake's shoreline. This is the heart of the lakeshore plain with nitrogen-rich, but well-drained soils that have to be tamed lest they produce too much fruit-shading greenery. The proximity of the water produces morning dew that, some argue, adds character to the wine. Autumn can linger for as much as two weeks longer than other areas of the peninsula due to the hot water-bottle effect of the lake. This longer season gives red varieties a significant boost.

STREWN WINERY AND WINE COUNTRY COOKING SCHOOL

From Highway 55 turn north (left going towards the village) and continue to the end. At Lakeshore Road, turn west, or left again. On the corner is Strewn Winery and Wine Country Cooking School. It was a dream come true for winemaker Joe Will and his wife, home economist and PR executive, Jane Langdon. The old canning factory had been empty for twenty-five years. No one else saw the possibilities that Will and Langdon could see.

In 1997, they opened their winery/cooking school with a vision to create a total winery experience that combined both culinary appreciation and wine appreciation. Will's wines, particularly his Chardonnays and Rieslings, have won him international recognition. The cooking school,

Strewn Winery and Wine Country Cooking School
1339 Lakeshore Road
Niagara-on-the-Lake, Ontario, L0S 1J0
Tel: 905-468-1229
Fax: 905-468-8305
E-mail: strewnwines@sympatico.ca
www.strewnwinery.com
Annual production: 15,000 cases
Located in an ingeniously renovated old canning factory, now the home of both the winery and the cooking school, with demo and participation kitchens. Fun!

Right: *Terroir La Cachette*

Terroir La Cachette
1339 Lakeshore Road
Niagara-on-the-Lake
Tel: 905-468-1222
Email: tricia@lachachette.com
www.lachachette.com

Sunnybrook Farm Estate Winery
R. R. #3
1425 Lakeshore Road
Niagara-on-the-Lake, Ontario, L0S 1J0
Tel: 905-468-1122
www.sunnybrookfarmwinery.com
For some of the best fruit wines in Ontario,
stop here. Delicious.

managed by Langdon, features a large demonstration kitchen, plus a magnificent hands-on kitchen for seminars and workshops. Appreciation classes are scheduled regularly. Perfect for individual or corporate outings and team building exercises. A restaurant now completes the package, opened in the fall of 2000.

TERROIR LA CACHETTE

Located within Strewn Winery, Terroir La Cachette is Patricia Keyes and Chef Alain Levesque's gift to Niagara. Chef Alain uses locally grown and raised products in his Provencal-styled menu. Although located within a winery, La Cachette allows visitors to taste other wines of the region. The dining room is lovely, with colourful décor and comfortable tables. It's one of the nicest places to dine at moderate prices in Niagara-on-the-Lake. Plan a trip to the winery and include Terroir La Cachette in your itinerary.

SUNNYBROOK FARM ESTATE WINERY

Yes, there is a Rebecca who makes the wines with her dad. This is a fruit wine operation producing some fruit wines of distinction and purity. I firmly believe there is a place for fruit wines in any wine-loving repertoire. Gerry Goertz, owner and winemaker, is able to capture the tree-ripened character of his fruit. A nice diversion from higher alcohol, grape-based wines.

KONZELMANN ESTATE WINERY

A few kilometres east is Konzelmann Estate, which was established in 1984 by Herbert Konzelmann, who found the site and soils of this lakeshore vineyard ideal for premium wines. Konzelmann had come from five generations of winemakers in Germany, but he chose Canada to start an operation where he could introduce new ideas in winegrowing and winemaking.

Konzelmann introduced the vertical training method to the region. This helps to achieve higher sugars while maintaining acids. He minimizes his use of chemicals in the vineyard and works to create wines of charm and easy drinking. He is noted for his cherry-ripe Pinot Noirs, tropical Chardonnays, soft Merlots, and incredibly rich Icewines.

STONECHURCH VINEYARDS

Rick and Fran Hunse joined the ranks of those diligent grape growers who moved from supplying top-quality grapes to other wineries to producing wines of their own. The winery is named after an old nineteenth-century stone church once near the corner of the Hunse farm. Legend has it that during Prohibition the farm's underground caves served as sanctuary for rumrunning smugglers.

They produce Cabernet Sauvignon, Cabernet Franc, Baco Noir, Pinot Noir, Chardonnay Riesling, Gewurztraminer, Icewine and Late Harvest wines. One of my favourites is their Morio Muscat — unique to Stonechurch Vineyards.

Konzelmann Estates Winery
R.R. #3
1096 Lakeshore Road
Niagara-on-the-Lake, Ontario, L0S 1J0
Tel: 905-935-2866
Fax: 905-935-2864
E-mail: konzelmannwines@konzelmann.com
www.konzelmannwines.com
Annual Production: 46,000 cases
Crisp, well-made Rieslings, ripe, tropical Chardonnays, voluptuous Icewines, fresh cherry Pinot Noirs and mellow Merlots. What better reason to stop?

Stonechurch Vineyards
R. R. #5
1270 Irvine Road
Niagara-on-the-Lake, Ontario, L0S 1J0
Tel: 905-935-3535
Fax: 905-646-8144
E-mail: wine@stonechurch.com
www.stonechurch.com
Annual Production: 55,000 cases
Interesting program of activities, including small theatre and stargazing barbecues. Try their Cabernet Franc and Morio Muscat.

ACCOMMODATIONS

Vintage Inns
(which include The Prince of Wales, Queen's Landing and The Pillar and Post)
155 Byron Street
Niagara-on-the-Lake, Ontario, L0S 1J0
Tel: 905-468-2195
Fax: 905-468-2227
www.vintageinns.com
These four-diamond hotels are all newly renovated and provide a luxurious stay in the heart of the village. Rates: $360-$1,000.

Left: *Stonechurch Vineyards*

ENTRE LACS — DAY TRIPS AROUND THE PENINSULA

The Niagara Wine Route is one of several connecting routes and recreation trails that encircle the peninsula in appealing ways — each with a slightly different focus. In Niagara-on-the-Lake the wine route ends (or begins, depending on your orientation), but it is also where one of the most romantic drives in Canada begins — the Niagara Parkway.

At Fort Erie, the Parkway's southern terminus, the Lake Erie Southerntier Drive begins, taking you westward around the southern portion of the Niagara Peninsula, through the beach side communities of Fort Erie, Ridgeway, Sherkston and Port Colborne. At Port Colborne the Welland Canals Interim Parkway completes the circle, connecting you northward with one of the world's most brilliant feats of engineering, the Welland Canal, whose system of locks — eight in all — lift oceangoing vessels "up the mountain" of the Niagara Escarpment, carrying them safely from one Great Lake to another.

THE NIAGARA PARKWAY

The stunning Niagara Parkway meanders beside the Niagara River in a peaceful 58-kilometre (36-mile) uninterrupted stretch. It is perfect picnic country, where you can supplement lunch with fresh fruits and vegetables from any one of the numerous farm market stands that line the route. Billed as the "Gateway to Canada," it is a road that evokes Ontario's living history.

Left: *Majestic Niagara Falls*   Top: *Niagara River, looking north*

Brock's Monument

PLACES OF INTEREST

Casino Niagara
5705 Falls Avenue
Niagara Falls, Ontario, L2G 7M9
Tel: 1-888-946-3255
Fax: 905-353-6731
Email: info@casinoniagara.com
discoveringniagara.com
At the Casino there are skill-testing table games, slot machines and 135 gaming tables including Blackjack, Caribbean Stud, Craps and Roulette. There are more than 2700 slot and video poker machines on four levels in denominations from nickels to $100. Dining opportunities range from the quick and casual (Hard Rock Cafe, Perks Café, The Market, Planet Hollywood) to fine dining (Twenty-One).

Hydrofoil Lake Jet Lines
10 Yonge Street, Suite 1111
Toronto, Ontario,
Tel: 416-214-4923

Maid of the Mist Boat Tours
5920 River Road
Niagara Falls, Ontario, L2E 6V6
Tel: 905-358-5781
Ride in the waters beneath the Falls.

From Niagara-on-the-Lake, the Parkway passes large farms, buildings and homes of architectural and historical significance.

It is a serene drive with dense woods climbing the banks of the river on one side. On the other, regal homes, both historic and contemporary, speak eloquently of two centuries of life in Niagara. Markers and monuments commemorate the history that was made along this river border, such as the monument in Queenston Heights Park to Laura Secord in memory of her heroic walk from Queenston to Beaverdams, 13.6 kilometres (8 miles) away, to warn the British of an impending American attack on their position. And, of course, the towering 50-metre (190-foot) monument to General Brock himself, who stands as a silent sentry on top of the Escarpment — a heroic talisman of Canada's determination to be sovereign.

Major General Brock lost his life on a cold morning in October of 1812, when American troops crossed the Niagara River before dawn. Landing at Queenston Heights, they attacked a British battery and took control of the British cannon, pointing it directly on Queenston. Brock immediately organized a counterattack, led the first charge and was shot in the heart. His second in command, Major General Sheaffe, eventually appeared behind the Americans, trapping them against the gorge and forcing them to surrender. By mid-morning, the British army had thwarted the invasion, but Upper Canada had lost a leader.

When Brock was placed in command of the army of Upper Canada in 1802 he rallied the Canadians to defend their country against Americans eager to add British North America to their borders. When the War of 1812 was over, Brock was first remembered by a high Tuscan column. In 1840 the column was blown up by a disgruntled member of Mackenzie's rebels. A new monument was dedicated on October 13, 1857, 45 years after Brock's death.

The panoramic view of the Niagara River from just below Brock's monument shows a sleepy river, exhausted and subdued by the high-energy workout it had had just moments before. Here it meanders gently through the orchards and vineyards of Niagara as if to put off its final entry into Lake Ontario at Niagara-on-the-Lake.

Paralleling the Parkway is a paved 2.5-metre (8-foot) recreation trail that is ideal for joggers, walkers, bicyclists, wheelchairists and bladers. It runs the entire length of the Parkway.

The Niagara Parkway is just one of the many treasures developed and maintained by the Niagara Parks Commission, the Crown Corporation founded in 1885 as a self-funding agency of the Ontario government to "preserve and enhance the natural beauty of the Falls and the Niagara River

corridor for the enjoyment of visitors while maintaining financial independence." It is one of the few parks in the world that operates without a deficit.

In the Niagara Parks there are 4,000 acres of manicured public parkland stretching along the entire length of the Niagara River from Fort Erie to Niagara-on-the-Lake, with golf courses restaurants, gift shops, flower gardens and conservatories, in addition to hundreds of acres of lawn and shade trees, boat-launching areas, covered picnic pavilions and picnic tables, nature trails and historic sites. It is clean and breathtakingly beautiful. You'll agree with Winston.

NIAGARA FALLS

The Niagara Parkway is the main "street" that eventually passes the Falls themselves. Expect traffic to be congested, so if you want to linger for a while, it's worth parking the car and travelling through town on the bus service they call the "People Movers," which travels between the Rapids View Parking Lot and Queenston Heights Park. One low fee allows you to travel a 30-kilometre (18-mile) loop, stopping at any of the Parks' attractions along the way.

Visiting Niagara Falls is a pilgrimage we make at least once in our life-

Top: *Niagara River looking south to whirlpool*

Above: *Cycling trails*

Spanish Aero Car ride

Niagara Spanish Aero Car
Niagara Parkway
Niagara Falls, Ontario, L3K 5X7
Tel: 905-371-0254
Ride hundreds of feet over the rapids.

Niagara Helicopters
3731 Victoria Avenue
Niagara Falls, Ontario, L2E 6V5
Tel: 905-357-5672
An exciting way to view the falls.

Oh Canada Eh?! Dinner Show
Tel: 905-374-1995 or 1-800-467-2071
Rave reviews.

Ride Niagara — The Ultimate Thrill
(Simulated and stunning)
Tel: 905-374-7433
Rainy day fun!

The Roselawn Complex (home to Showboat Festival Theatre, Arts)
296 Fielden Avenue
Port Colborne, Ontario, L3K 5X7
Tel: 905-834-7572 or 905-834-0833
Theatre in the round. Great value.

time. Our reasons vary from the spiritual to the sentimental. We go to be mesmerized, inspired and humbled — to feel the spray, to witness its explosion of power and noise from the safe side of the rail, to pay our respects. It's good for the soul. Although the shrines along this pilgrims' route are not grand cathedrals in which to recast the tempo and purpose of our lives, there are some captivating pleasures worth exploring.

Some highlights include the Butterfly Conservatory, where you can enjoy 2,000 free-flying butterflies all year long in a rainforest setting. You may want to save this visit for a cooler afternoon. If the day is hot and humid, take the Journey Behind the Falls. You'll get a welcomed drenching, but there's also something thrilling about being so close to the base of the Falls, yet so safe. It's a thunderous nearness that vibrates the bones.

Of all the attractions at the Falls, it is the Glen that invites you to share the primeval secrets of the Falls themselves. The parking lot to the Glen is located on the Niagara Parkway just 3 kilometres (2 miles) below the Falls. In order to reach the Glen, you have to descend a winding precipitous path from the cliffs above, so wear good walking shoes. Each step you take brings you 8,000 years closer to the genesis of the river's ancient bed. There are jumbles of boulders, narrow passageways, forest-cool paths, pot holes, teetering rocks and over fifty species of wildflowers on its 4 kilometres (2.5 miles) of paths. It is second only to the Falls in natural, Carolinian Zone beauty.

The Niagara Parks Commission, from the very beginning, realized the importance of trees, shrubs and flowers for the future of the Parks' development. Today, the Niagara Parks are known for their elaborate gardens, manicured lawns, restful vistas and ornamental displays. To have high-quality plants available, the Parks grow their own in a 522.5-metre (5,625-foot) structure, where they propagate unusual species and varieties of flowers. Visiting the greenhouse is a gardener's delight.

The Parks' gardens are also a source of inspiration, particularly the Botanical Gardens and grounds that surround the School of Horticulture, nine miles north of the Falls. Visitors can visit a variety of self-guided tours of herb, vegetable, rose and lilac gardens, plus a gracious arboretum with labelled collections of several hundred trees and shrubs.

A little-known horticultural feature is the Parks' fragrance garden, located north of the Niagara Parks Greenhouse. The garden is at its best in summer and is popular with the visually handicapped. There are over 100 different species of plants known for their texture and aroma, including sage, thyme, rosemary, heliotrope, linden and rose.

Of the attractions outside the Parks, one of my favourites is the IMAX® Theatre, located minutes from the Falls. This giant six-storey movie screen shows some remarkable film footage in a comfortable theatre setting.

SOUTH OF THE FALLS

After the Parkway leaves the Falls, the character of the countryside changes. The trees that climbed the steep banks of the river near Niagara-on-the-Lake give way to a more approachable shoreline. The river's tilt towards Lake Ontario is less abrupt, thus creating quieter, more navigable waters. The uninitiated might even think the waters placid, but as many can attest who have made the crossing to the United States by boat, the six-mile an hour current can quickly overpower arms tired from rowing and carry a light craft precipitously close to the rapids that precede the river's drop over the Escarpment.

On the banks of Black Creek, is a century-and-a-half-old pub that was once a stop on the old Tally Ho four-horse coach line, The Lighthouse Restaurant and Pub. It is midway between Niagara Falls and Fort Erie and is a great stop for a brew and a snack or dinner.

Creek banks also held great promise for thousands of Black fugitive slaves who were guided to Upper Canada, where slavery had been abolished since 1793, during the early part of the nineteenth century. Bertie Hall, on the Parkway, was said to be used as a safe house for freedom seekers who made the crossing. A Niagara's Freedom Trail plaque on the grounds details the history of the building, which now houses a fascinating collection of

Niagara Parks Butterfly Conservatory
Niagara Parkway
Niagara Falls, Ontario
Tel: 905-371-0254
Thousands of live, exotic butterflies; a very popular destination.

Journey Behind the Falls
905-371-0254
Slicker-covered 1.5 kilometre walk through the caves under the Falls; watch the mighty waters fall from above.

Niagara Parks Botanical Gardens
Niagara Parkway
Niagara Falls, Ontario
Tel: 905-371-0254
Gorgeous gardens and floral displays.

Niagara Parks Greenhouse
Niagara Parkway
Niagara Falls, Ontario
Tel: 905-371-0254
Propagations of indigenous and exotic plants that the Parks Commission uses in its gardens.

Niagara Parks Butterfly Conservatory

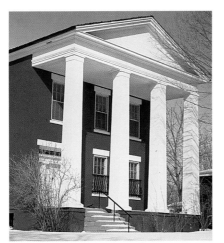

Mildred M. Mahoney Dolls' House Museum

Niagara Falls IMAX Theatre
6170 Buchanan Avenue
Niagara Falls, Ontario, L2G 7T8
Tel: 905-358-3611
Mammoth screen; reasonably priced.

FESTIVALS AND EVENTS

Welland Rose Festival and Lobsterfest
June (usually first week)
Tel: 905-732-6603
www.rosefestival.on.ca

Showboat Festival Theatre
Roselawn Complex
296 Fielden Avenue
Port Colborne, Ontario, L3K 5X7
From June to September
Box office: 905-834-0833

Friendship Festival
Fort Erie/Buffalo international celebration
First week in July
Tel: 1-888-333-1987
www.friendshipfestival.com

dollhouses — the Mildred M. Mahoney Collection. This is not a toy stop for the kids. The houses are miniature replicas of sixteenth, seventeenth, and eighteenth-century European manors, made by aristocratic women of the manors, down to the most intricate details. Fascinating.

Slightly north of Fort Erie on the American shore opposite the southern head of Grand Island is Navy Island where, in 1837, William Lyon Mackenzie and his cohort Samuel Chandler made a daring escape from the armed forces of Upper Canada that had come to arrest Mackenzie. He led a small but growing rebel community that sought to replace the existing government consisting of a rather self-serving and rigid conservative political elite — the Family Compact — with more democratic practices. Once in American territory on Navy Island, Mackenzie proclaimed a new provisional government for Upper Canada.

To quell what was perceived as a serious threat to political stability, Upper Canada sent forces to blockade the island, where they ill-advisedly cut loose an American ship that had been providing supplies to Mackenzie, then set it ablaze — a clear violation of American sovereignty. In reprisal, the Americans torched a Canadian steamer, setting off what could have been another international conflict, but cooler heads prevailed and negotiated an end to hostilities. Without sufficient mainland support to continue, Mackenzie admitted the futility of his cause and moved to Buffalo.

Several spots along the Parkway are noteworthy for being the best places in North America from which to watch gulls. The fast-flowing waters of the Niagara River regularly attract nineteen different species of gulls along the shore. Several spots along the river are ideal — the head of the river near Lake Erie, and the mouth at Lake Ontario; the Falls and the rapids just above and below the Falls; the barge, the Whirlpool, the power stations and down river at Queenston.

THE LAKE ERIE SOUTHERNTIER DRIVE

The Niagara Parkway ends at the Peace Bridge in Fort Erie, a city probably more familiar to Americans than it is to most Canadians. This is America's port of entry to Canada from Buffalo via the Peace Bridge. In summer, thousands of day-trippers stream across the bridge to bask on the beautiful beaches of Lake Erie's north shore. This is where the Lake Erie Southerntier Drive begins — a dogleg to the west at Fort Erie that passes through the hamlets of Ridgeway and several beach-side communities. The scenic drive follows Highway 1 (Dominion Road) out of Fort Erie, paralleling the busier Highway 3 (Garrison Road) to Ridge Road, where it turns south to Farr (which becomes Michener). It then takes a turn to the northwest at Sherkston Road, just north of Point Abino, then west onto Killaly Road straight to Port Colborne. Several golf courses, marinas, campgrounds and waterfront parks line the route.

FORT ERIE

Because of its strategic location at the head of the Niagara River, the British built a fort here in 1764, first as a defence against Native attacks, then, because they were a cannon shot away from Buffalo, New York, as a bastion against invading Americans. The original fort, and its successor, were destroyed by ice that slammed onto shore from the lake. Shortly after the next fort was built a little farther south, and before it was complete, it saw considerable action during the War of 1812. Although the Americans captured it in the summer of 1814, the reversals of war caused the occupying U.S. commander to withdraw to Buffalo, but not before blowing up the fort. This third fort was restored in 1937. Re-enactments of the siege take place every summer.

Fort Erie, like the eleven other municipalities in the greater region of Niagara, is both the name of the City of Fort Erie as well as the umbrella name of the town under which several distinct settlements were amalgamated in 1970. Fort Erie is also home to several museums, including a railroad museum, an antique firefighting museum and the Ridgeway Battlefield Museum. The Fort Erie Race Track is also nearby with harness racing held weekdays from mid-May to August.

Follow Highway 1 as it leaves the historic Fort Erie to continue on the (8-mile) Lake Erie Southerntier Drive. Turn south at any point along the highway and you'll reach the highlight of the drive, a 13.6-kilometre paved recreational pathway called the Friendship Trail. The trail starts near Kraft Road (on Edgemere Road), the birthplace of Mr. Kraft of Kraft cheese fame, and travels due west through twelve sections (each adopted by a different local school) to Gorham Road and the Crystal Beach Trail Entrance.

The Friendship Trail passes through the charming town of Ridgeway, a perfect spot for an ice cream or lunch at Ridgeway's Restaurant on Ridge Road, the main street. The Trail is a peaceful diversion, plus it's a wonderful opportunity to get some fresh air, exercise and have a little talk with nature. Return to Highway 1 until you reach Sherkston Road, a northwest approach to Highway 3 for a short stint, then turn left onto Killaly Street to Port Colborne, the Canal City.

Niagara Food Festival
Merritt Island, Welland, Ontario
End of September
Tel: 905-735-4832
www.tourismniagara.com/welland

Oktoberfest
first week in October
Port Colborne, Ontario
Tel: 905-835-2901
www.portcolborne.com

Loch Sloy Highland Games
Fort Erie, Ontario
Mid-June at Historic Fort Erie
905-871-7152 or 1-877-642-7275
lochsloy@vaxxine.com

ACCOMMODATIONS

BED AND BREAKFASTS
(www.tourismniagara.com)

Cairngorm
5395 River Road
Niagara Falls, Ontario, L2E 3H1
Tel: 905-354-4237
Fax: 905-354-9816
E-mail: cairngorm@sympatico.ca
Rates: $100 - $140

Niagara Riverview
21 Cairns Crescent
Service Road 4
Niagara Parkway
Fort Erie, Ontario, L2A 5M4
Tel: 905-871-0865
E-mail: bed&breakfast@forterie.com

Bedham Hall Bed and Breakfast
4835 River Road
Niagara Falls, Ontario, L2E 3G4
Tel: 905-374-8515
Fax: 905-374-9189
E-mail: bedhambb@cgocable.net

HOTELS, INNS AND COTTAGE RENTALS

Niagara Falls, Canada Visitor & Convention Bureau
5515 Stanley Avenue
Niagara Falls, Ontario, L2G 3X4
Tel: 905-356-6061 or 1-800-563-2557
http://tourismniagara.com/nfcvcb

Niagara Parks Commission
7400 Portage Road South
Niagara Falls, Ontario, L2E 6X8
Tel: 905-356-2241
Fax: 905-356-9237
www.niagaraparks.com

COTTAGE RENTALS

Long Beach Rentals
905-899-3308

Sherkston Shores
1-800-263-8121

THE NIAGARA PARKWAY

RESTAURANTS

Casa Mia Italian Restaurant
3518 Portage Road
Niagara Falls, Ontario, L2J 2K4
Tel: 905-356-5410
Italian cuisine at its finest. Momma still oversees the kitchen while son Claudio cooks. Moderate prices.

Port Colborne

The historic canal town of Port Colborne is the southern entrance to the Welland Canal at Lock 8 — one of the longest locks in the world. An elevated observation stand provides an excellent viewing deck. Cross the canal and turn south to West Street, an historic shopping area bordering the canal that dates back to the 1800s. For marine buffs, the Historical and Marine Museum is an interesting visit. This five-building complex features a canal display, an operating blacksmith's shop, log school house and a tea room.

Also in Port Colborne is a multi-million dollar marina at Sugarloaf Harbour and Restaurant, great for a waterside lunch. A local favourite restaurant, however, is Lucy's Café. Lucy cooks southern Italian in a ten-table bistro on Nickel Street. Food's terrific, but it's not for the faint of appetite.

For the heck of it, drive to Lakeshore Road for an optical illusion you won't forget — the Shrinking Mill. The closer you get, the smaller it gets. (Take Cement Plant Road south to Lakeshore Road, turn east and look straight ahead as you approach.)

While in Port Colborne be sure to check the playbill at the Showboat Festival Theatre located at the Roselawn Complex on Fielden Avenue. It is quite an active summer theatre.

The Welland Canal Corridor

Complete the Greater Niagara Circle Tour by taking the Welland Canals Parkway Interim Route. Although the route does not completely run adjacent to the canal (yet), an interim signed driving route has been established that spans the entire north-south corridor. The present route zigzags its way north but it's not hard to follow.

From Lock 8 and Fountainview Park, go north on Welland Street to Main Street East (Highway 3), turn west to Elm Street, continue on Elm to Forks Road, turn east for a short stint to Kingsway, where you'll turn north onto Ontario for a short zig, then zag north again onto King Street and follow King to East Main. This will take you into the City of Welland, where you can view the giant mural display on many of the walls of the city's downtown buildings. Time for lunch? Dinner? Rinderlin's on Bulgar Street is very fine.

Leave Welland by going north on Niagara Street, then east on Woodlawn Road to Highway 406. This highway will lead you to the famous Twinned Flight Locks 4,5,6 and 7, located in Thorold. Exit at Beaverdams Road and follow the signs to the Welland Canal. (Take Beaverdams Road to Portland Street, then turn east onto Chapel. Turn north, then make a quick right (east) to the bridge that links up with Government Road.)

The exciting thing about going to the canal is being able to get close to enormous vessels from all over the world, then watching them "lifted" like rubber ducks in a bath through a series of locks 100 metres (326 feet) high over the cliff face of the Niagara Escarpment — the same cliff that the the Niagara River falls over. Until the canal was built, originally in 1829, the Niagara Gorge and the Falls were impassable obstacles to shipping. Goods had to be unloaded from ships and loaded onto wagons at Queenston, then transported over the Portage Road to Chippawa.

Now, miraculously, water does the work. The locks are filled and emptied by water flowing downhill from Lake Erie toward Lake Ontario. The average lift of each lock is about 14.2 metres (46.5 feet).

Another favourite spot to view this brilliant feat of engineering is at Lock 3 at the Welland Canals Centre located at the St. Catharines Historical Museum. Here you can stand nose-to-nose with deck hands and captains. Nice spot for lunch, too, with gift shop, audio-visual presentation and ample free parking. Located here is part of the completed paved trail of a proposed Greater Niagara Circle Route linking up with the Welland Canal Multi-Use Trail. Great for biking, hiking or blading alongside these floating behemoths as they inch their way through the channel.

To complete the tour from Lock 3 in St. Catharines, take Government Road, which parallels the canal. This will take you to the QEW, where the Garden City Skyway crosses the Welland Canal, and home again.

Delduca's Italian Restaurant
4781 Portage Road
Niagara Falls, Ontario, L2E 6B1
Tel: 905-357-3638
The best sandwiches and salads in Niagara.
Excellent value.

Farfalle
Casino Niagara, 5705 Falls Street
Niagara Falls, Ontario, L2G 7M9
Tel: 905-374-9122 or 888-946-3255
Elegant dining Casino style. Upscale.

Frank's Tomato Pie
6869 Lundy's Lane
Niagara Falls, Ontario, L2G 1V7
Tel: 905-371-9111
Hip and happening. Delicious soups.
Moderate prices.

The Lighthouse Restaurant and Pub
4301 Niagara Parkway
Stevensville, Ontario, L0S 1S0
Tel: 905-382-4513
Located on the Niagara River. Huge portions; pub style. Excellent value.

Mama Leone
5705 Victoria Street
Niagara Falls, Ontario, L2G 3L5
Tel: 905-357-5220
Northern Italian dining. Very fine wine list.
Moderate to upscale.

Queenston Heights Restaurant
Niagara Parkway (Queenston)
Queenston, Ontario, L0S 1L0
Tel: 1-877-642-7275
Brunch or lunch to enjoy the belle view of the Niagara River. Fine dining.

Rainbow Dining Room
Skyline Brock Hotel
5685 Falls Avenue
Niagara Falls, Ontario, L2G 6W7
Tel: 905-374-4444 or 1-800-263-7135
Newly renovated; spectacular view of the falls. Moderate to upscale.

CABERNET AND FRIENDS TOUR

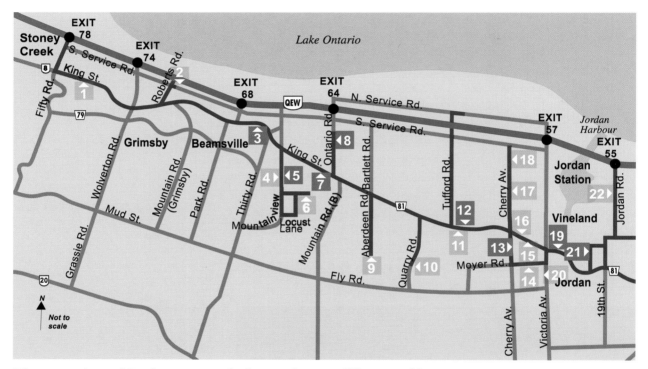

The great wines of Bordeaux are made from Cabernet Sauvignon, Cabernet Franc and Merlot. Who would have thought that Niagara, best known for whites, could produce very fine Bordeaux varieties? Well, pioneering growers, that's who!

When they realized that Niagara has more critical sunshine hours during the growing season than Bordeaux, they took the plunge and planted. Today, the following producers excel in these age-worthy varieties of inherent complexity. Each produce separate bottlings of the specific variety plus a blend of two or three. You can taste the purity of the 100% varietal wine and then compare the complexity of the blend.

WESTERN NIAGARA

- Peninsula Ridge Estates (3)
- Thirty Bench Vineyard and Winery (5)
- Daniel Lenko Estate Winery (7)
- Magnotta (8)
- Thomas and Vaughan Vintners (12)
- Lakeview Cellars (13)
- Stoney Ridge Cellars (19)
- Cave Spring Cellars (21)

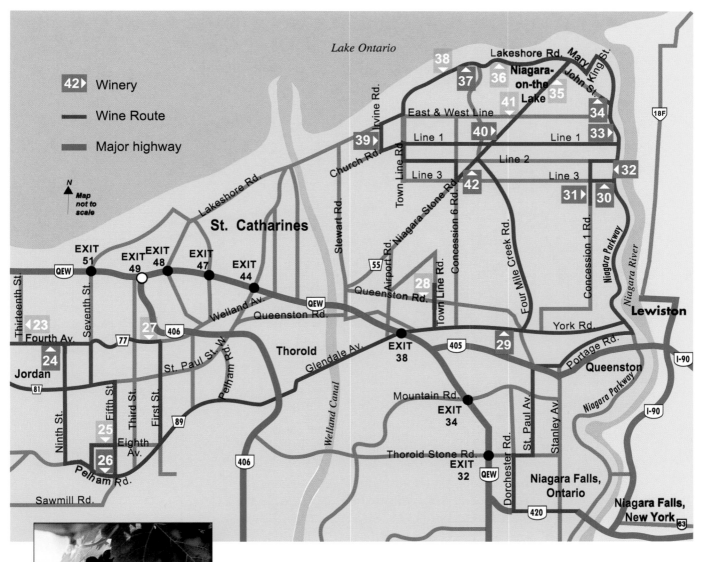

42▶ Winery

—— Wine Route

■ Major highway

N
Map not to scale

Lake Ontario

St. Catharines

Jordan

Thorold

Niagara-on-the Lake

Lewiston

Queenston

Niagara Falls, Ontario

Niagara Falls, New York

EASTERN NIAGARA
- Creekside Estate Winery (24)
- Henry of Pelham Family Estate Winery (26)
- Château des Charmes (29)
- Inniskillin Wines (30)
- Marynissen Estates (31)

- Reif Estate Winery (32)
- Lailey Vineyards (33)
- Peller Estates Winery (34)
- Strewn Winery (37)
- Stonechurch Vineyards (39)
- Pillitteri Estates Winery (40)
- Hillebrand Estates Winery (42)

CHARDONNAY TOUR

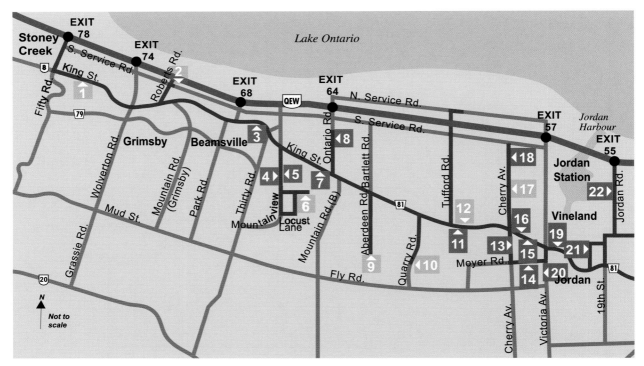

You can put any of the following Chardonnays from Niagara against any other international Chardonnay matched style for style, price for price, and my prediction is you will prefer the one from Niagara. Niagara's Chardonnays are second to none.

WESTERN NIAGARA
- Peninsula Ridge Estates (3)
- Angels Gate Winery (4)
- Thirty Bench Vineyard and Winery (5)
- Daniel Lenko Estate Winery (7)

- Magnotta (8)
- Malivoire Wine Company (11)
- Lakeview Cellars (13)
- Vineland Estates (14)
- Kacaba Vineyards (15)
- Willow Heights Estate Winery (16)
- Birchwood Estate Wines (18)
- Stoney Ridge Cellars (19)
- Featherstone Estate Winery and Vineyard (20)
- Cave Spring Cellars (21)
- Harbour Estates Winery (non-oaked) (22)

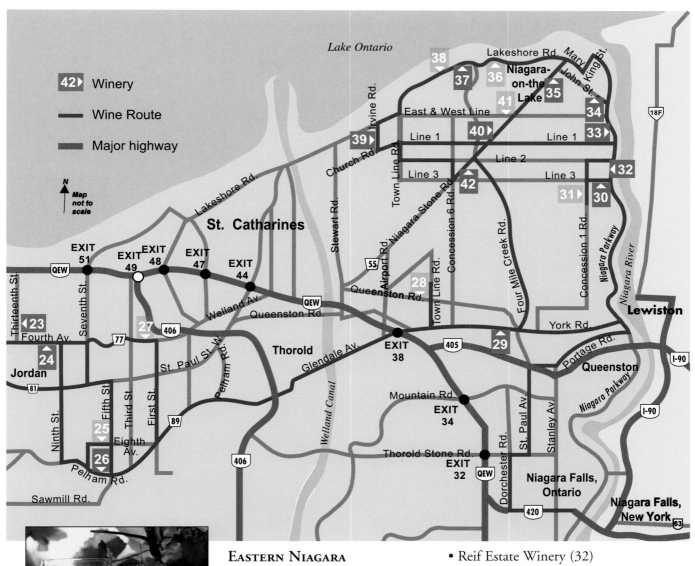

42▶ Winery

— Wine Route

■ Major highway

Eastern Niagara

- Thirteenth Street Winery: Sandstone (23)
- Creekside Estate Winery (24)
- Henry of Pelham Family Estate Winery (26)
- Château des Charmes (29)
- Inniskillin Wines (30)
- Reif Estate Winery (32)
- Lailey Vineyards (33)
- Peller Estates Winery (34)
- Jackson-Triggs Vintners (35)
- Strewn Winery (37)
- Stonechurch Vineyards (39)
- Pillitteri Estates Winery (40)
- Hillebrand Estates Winery (42)

ICEWINE TOUR

The best icewine in the world, without equivocation, is made in Canada. Icewines from Niagara are the benchmark against which all others are measured. What fun to determine benchmarks of your own. Since the two most common varieties from which icewines are made are Vidal and Riesling, set out and compare the two at different properties.

Vidal icewines are more exuberant — like cheerleaders, upfront, vivacious and bold. On the other hand, Rieslings are usually more restrained, more studious, like fine lace with filament flavours that together create a longer-lived wine of complexity. The following wineries make both Vidal and Rieslings. You be the judge.

At Inniskillin look for treats such as Dornfelder, Cabernet Franc, and Chenin Blanc, an oak-aged and a sparkling icewine. Jackson-Triggs also produces a delightful Gewurztraminer icewine. Other wineries that excel in Vidal are Reif, Konzelmann, and Stonechurch on the Niagara-on-the-Lake side. Towards the Bench, Lakeview Cellars, Magnotta, Vineland Estates, EastDell, Peninsula Ridge, Stoney Ridge Estates, Thomas and Vaughan, and Willow Heights produce delightful comparisons.

On the Bench side of the Peninsula, more prize-winning wines come from Royal de Maria, Cave Spring Cellars, Harvest Estates, and Henry of Pelham. Hernder Estate also produces one of the very few Pinot Gris icewines.

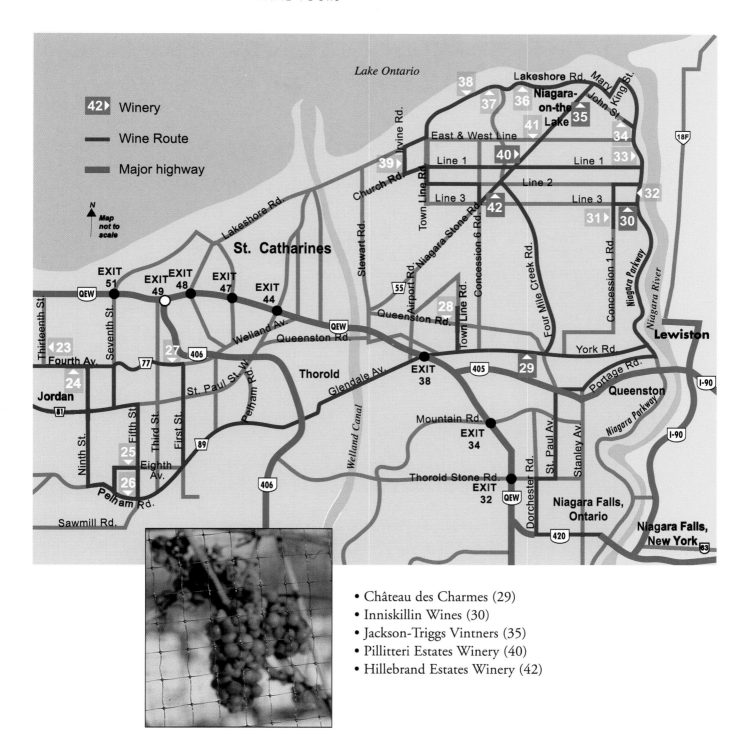

- Château des Charmes (29)
- Inniskillin Wines (30)
- Jackson-Triggs Vintners (35)
- Pillitteri Estates Winery (40)
- Hillebrand Estates Winery (42)

Pinot Noir Tour

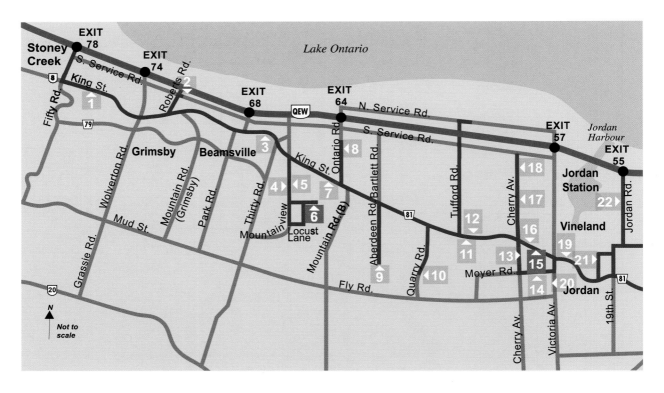

Pinot Noir is the great grape of Burgundy. Boisset, Burgundy's largest producer of fine wine, and Michel Picard, another esteemed negotiant and producer, have both recognized Niagara as having potential to produce outstanding Pinot Noir. Both French producers have invested in planting vineyards in Niagara. Le Clos Jordan, the Boisset/Vincor partnership, for example, is slated to open before 2005 with a facility designed by prominent architect Frank Gehry (Guggenheim Museum). To get a glimpse of what these French connoisseurs discovered, try the Pinot Noir at any of the following:

Western Niagara

- EastDell Estates (6)
- Kacaba Vineyards (15)

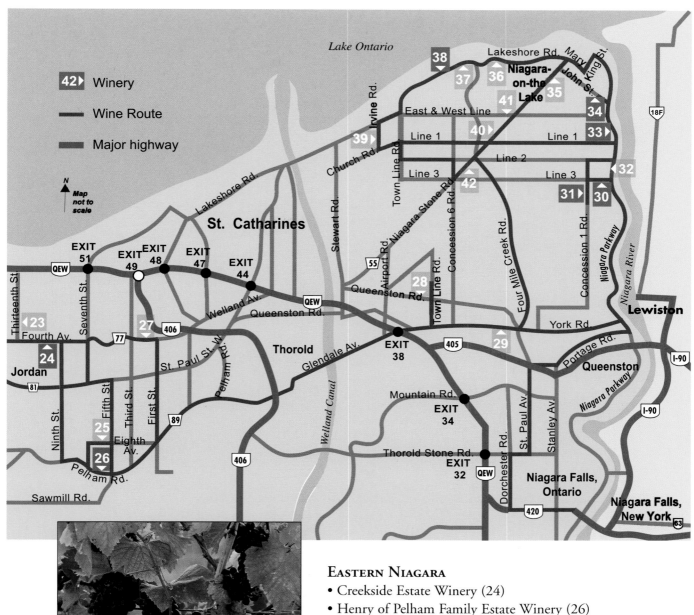

42▶ Winery

—— Wine Route

—— Major highway

Lake Ontario

N ↑ *Map not to scale*

38

37 **36** **Niagara-on-the Lake** **35**

41 **34**

East & West Line

39▶ **40▶** Line 1 Line 1 **33▶**

Church Rd.

Line 2

Line 3 **42** Line 3 **32**

Irvine Rd.

31▶ **30**

Town Line Rd.

Niagara Stone Rd.

Concession 6 Rd.

Four Mile Creek Rd.

Concession 1 Rd.

Niagara Parkway

Niagara River

St. Catharines

Stewart Rd.

Airport Rd.

18F

EXIT 51 **EXIT 49** **EXIT 48** **EXIT 47** **EXIT 44**

Thirteenth St.

Seventh St.

QEW

55

23 Fourth Av.

24

Jordan

77 **27** **406**

Lewiston

Queenston Rd.

QEW Queenston Rd.

28

Town Line Rd.

York Rd.

Portage Rd.

Queenston

I-90

St. Paul St. W.

Welland Av.

Thorold

Glendale Av.

EXIT 38 **405**

29

Fifth St.

Third St.

First St.

Pelham Rd.

81

89

25

Eighth Av.

26

Ninth St.

Pelham Rd.

406

Welland Canal

Mountain Rd.

EXIT 34

St. Paul Av.

Stanley Av.

I-90

Niagara Parkway

Niagara Falls, Ontario

Sawmill Rd.

Thorold Stone Rd.

EXIT 32 **QEW**

Dorchester Rd.

420

Niagara Falls, New York

83

Eastern Niagara
- Creekside Estate Winery (24)
- Henry of Pelham Family Estate Winery (26)
- Inniskillin Wines (30)
- Marynissen Estates (31)
- Lailey Vineyards (33)
- Peller Estates Winery (34)
- Konzelmann Estate Winery (38)

RIESLING TOUR

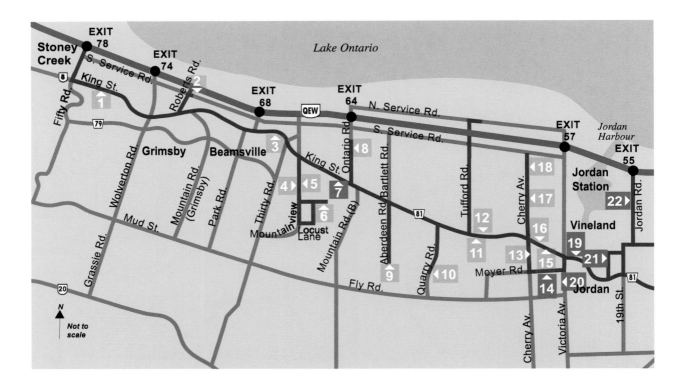

There is no question in my mind — Riesling is the king of white wines. Its sheer purity and power make this noble variety a classic. As cliché as it is, Rieslings are grown, not made, and Niagara grows some of the finest in the world. Niagara's Rieslings are like Victoria's Secret —known only to the adventurous and bold in heart. It's hard not to find a good one in Niagara, but choose from some of my favourites.

WESTERN NIAGARA

- Daniel Lenko Estate Winery (7)
- Vineland Estates (14)
- Stoney Ridge Cellars (19)
- Featherstone Estate Winery and Vineyard (20)
- Cave Spring Cellars (21)
- Harbour Estates Winery (22)

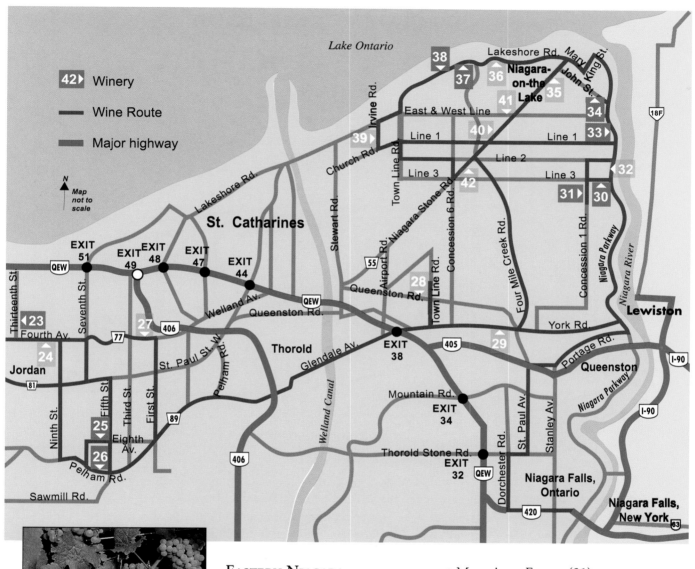

42▶ Winery

— Wine Route

— Major highway

Lake Ontario

N
Map not to scale

EASTERN NIAGARA
• Thirteenth Street: Funk (23)
• Hernder Estate Winery (25)
• Henry of Pelham Family Estate Winery (26)
• Inniskillin Wines (30)

• Marynissen Estates (31)
• Lailey Vineyard (33)
• Peller Estates Winery (34)
• Strewn Winery (37)
• Konzelmann Estate Winery (38)

SPECIALTY WINE TOUR

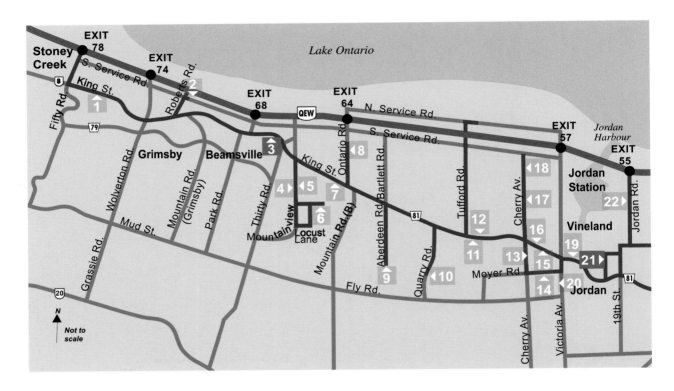

Zinfandel in Niagara? Semillon or Chenin Blanc? You bet! Would you believe Shiraz or an oak-aged apple wine that could fool the socks off your Chardonnay-loving friends? Yes, many producers are finding success with each of the above. Be the first to try any of the following:

- Fruit Wines: Sunnybrook Farms (36)
- Semillon and Chenin Blanc: Cave Spring Cellars (21)
- Shiraz: Inniskillin Wines (30), Peninsula Ridge Estates (3), Cave Spring Cellars (21)
- Zinfandel: Reif Estate Winery (32)

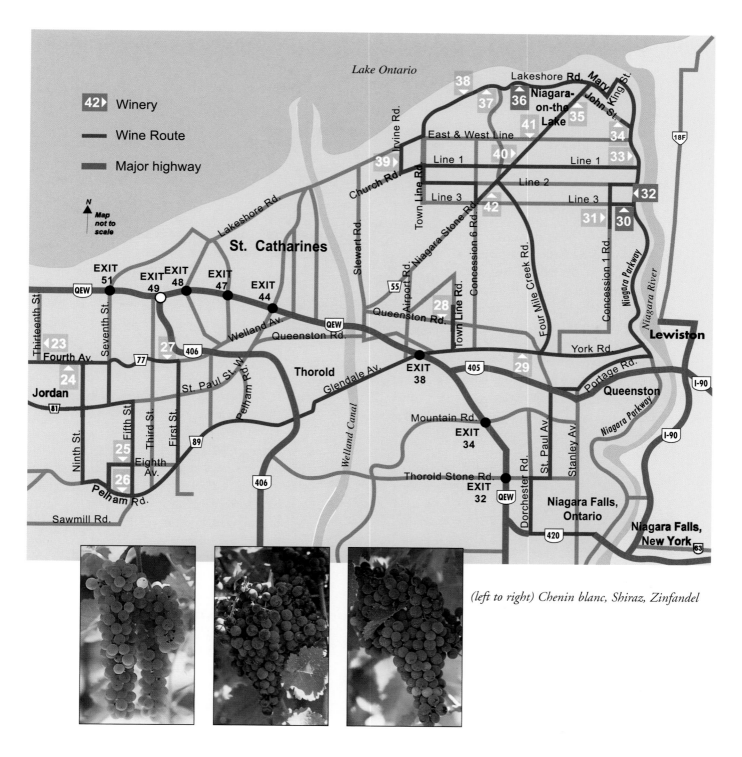

42 ▶ Winery

━━━ Wine Route

━━━ Major highway

N
▲ Map
not to
scale

Lake Ontario

Niagara-on-the-Lake

St. Catharines

Lewiston

Jordan

Thorold

Queenston

Niagara Falls, Ontario

Niagara Falls, New York

(left to right) Chenin blanc, Shiraz, Zinfandel

Top Ten Must See Wineries

Western Niagara

Malivoire Wine Company (11)

Film special effects producer, Martin Malivoire, took great pride to build a winery that uses the least invasive operation he could create: the less handling the better. At Malivoire, discover one of the most innovative gravity-fed systems in North America, and then taste the results of such care.

Vineland Estates (14)

This is the perfect wine country destination: a magnificent view of Lake Ontario, very fine dining, a captivating retail wine store and fabulous wines. A Niagara must. It's so popular among international dignitaries that they had to build a helicopter pad to accommodate demand.

Peninsula Ridge Estates (3)

Besides the historic home in which the restaurant is housed, the property is a stellar showcase of the most current technology on the market capable of shepherding wines in delicate European directions. The murals in the barrel cellar were painted by local artist Brian Romagnoli, recognized by the Queen of England for his veracity and gentleness of style.

Cave Spring Cellars (21)

This is more than wine —- it's food, shopping, galleries, historic artifacts, agricultural relics, and a rural setting overlooking a United Nations–sanctioned protected biosphere. It is understated elegance and old Niagara charm. There is nothing quite like the little hamlet of Jordan anywhere else in Ontario.

Henry of Pelham Family Estate Winery (26)

Henry of Pelham gets on the top ten list because of their extremely fine wines, and because they also offer a more casual alternative to wine country dining. In their coach house, you can buy lunches, picnics or light suppers to take with you or eat anywhere on their shaded patio or vineyard.

EASTERN NIAGARA:

Inniskillin Wines (30)

Inniskillin is the granddaddy of the modern Ontario wine industry, and with their experience has come wisdom. Here you'll find an outstanding self-paced, self-guided tour of the winery. Although expert help or the option for a guided tour are never too far away, it is a must stop for the enthusiast who wants to know more on his or her own time, space, and pace. Educator Debi Pratt guides the program and inventive pioneer Donald Ziraldo, co-founder of Inniskillin, inspires it further. His book *Anatomy of a Vineyard* is a welcomed complement to the experience.

Peller Estates Winery (34)

Go to this exquisite facility to taste the wine experience of a Niagara-cuisine lunch on the patio or dining room, or to buy wine accessories in their lavish winery retail store. Many of the ultra-premium wines sold at the estate are unavailable elsewhere, which provides added incentive to visit this extraordinary property.

Hillebrand Estates Winery (42)

Hillebrand is a treat and the tour covers all the bases. The winery retail store has gadgets and accessories to tantalize, but the spotlight is shared by the Hillebrand Vineyard Café and the delights of celebrity chef Tony de Luca. His humility belies his genius with wine and food pairings, and the service is exemplary.

Château des Charmes (29)

This is the architectural dream fulfilled of pioneer winemaker Paul Bosc Senior. Learn about *terroir* from these French-born and educated masters. With several blocks that they vinify separately, you can taste the difference "place" makes.

Strewn Winery (37)

As West Coast wine writer Matt Kramer once wrote, "The meaning of wine is food and the meaning of food is wine." Winemaker Joe Will and his wife Jane Langdon collaborate at Strewn, he in the cellar and she in their ultra-modern cooking school. Attached to the property is Le Terroir de Cachette, a beautiful wine country bistro — a little bit of Provençe in Niagara.

Glossary of Terms

Bench:

In the central portion of the Niagara Peninsula between Twelve Mile Creek and Thirty Mile Creek the Niagara Escarpment is lower, about 62 metres/200 feet high, and forms two broad terraces or ramps; that slope gently towards Lake Ontario. Because of the slope, the soils (carbonates and sandstones, limestone and shale), and the passive barrier of the escarpment acting as a rampart against offshore winds are circulated, this is a prime grape growing region of Ontario. Often referred to as the Beamsville Bench.

Carolinian Zone:

The northern subsection of the eastern deciduous forest zone characterized by more rare species of plants and animals than in any other part of Canada; plants and animals are more typical of the Carolinas in the US; particularly rich environment for a large variety of birds and mammals; more rare and endangered species found here than any other place in Canada.

Clone:

Vines that have been propagated from cuttings or buds from a single 'mother vine' resulting in plants that are genetically identical to the mother vine.

Kame:

A mound of stratified sediment laid down by surface water as an ice sheet melts; see Fonthill Kame in Pelham.

Labrusca:

Species of the Vitis genus native to North America; wine made from the juice of its grapes usually has a pronounced flavour often referred to as foxy; in this case, not a trait to be desired.

Niagara Escarpment:

A land form known as a cuesta or a ridge composed of rock layers with a slope on one side and a steep cliff on the other; the outer rim of a large saucer-shaped shoreline of an ancient lake, Lake Iroquois out of which the Great Lakes remained; rises near Rochester, N.Y., and runs eastward through the Niagara Peninsula paralleling the southern shore of Lake Ontario; continues to Hamilton where it turns north and continues to the Bruce Peninsula, crossing westward across northern Michigan and down west into the state of Wisconsin; declared a World Biosphere Reserve by the United Nations in 1990 because of its rare ecosystem.

Vinifera:

The European species of Vitis that comprises the classic varieties most used in wine production; vinifera is one of about 60 other species of the Vitis genus; can produce wine of exceptional quality.

Index